Leonard W. Riley

Jan., 1917

232.8

The Divinity of Christ in the
Gospel of John

The Divinity of Christ
In the Gospel of John

By
A. T. ROBERTSON, M.A., D.D., LL.D.
Professor of New Testament Interpretation in the Southern Baptist Theological Seminary, Louisville, Ky.

"The Word became flesh and dwelt among us."

NEW YORK   CHICAGO   TORONTO
Fleming H. Revell Company
LONDON   AND   EDINBURGH

New York: 158 Fifth Avenue
Chicago: 17 North Wabash Ave.
Toronto: 25 Richmond Street, W.
London: 21 Paternoster Square
Edinburgh: 100 Princes Street

To

Mrs. Mary Seaton Cary

like the Marys of this Gospel
Helpful Friend of Many Preachers

Preface

THE Gospel of John has fascinated me for over thirty years. The invitation to speak on it for a week to the Sunday-school teachers of Atlanta in October induced me to write out the five addresses in the hope that other Sunday-school teachers and ministers might at least be stimulated to a fresh study of this most wonderful book in all the world. There are all sorts of books about the Gospel of John and a brief bibliography is appended at the end of this volume. I do not undertake to write a full commentary on John's Gospel, but rather to develop the thesis of the book, as I understand it, with brevity and clearness so that the average man may understand the book better as a whole and in detail as he is led to read it with new interest. John can help us to see Jesus and thus to see God. It is just this vision of God in Christ that makes life worth while and rich. This is a good time for us all to say to Jesus in our hearts, " My Lord and my God."

A. T. R.

Louisville, Ky.

7

Contents

I

PRELIMINARY POINTS

" We know that his witness is true."

1. The Author.

A MYSTERY hangs over the authorship of the Fourth Gospel that may never be completely removed. For some reason the writer repeatedly speaks of " the disciple whom Jesus loved" and never mentions by name the Apostle John, though he does speak of " the *sons* of Zebedee " (John 21 : 2) as two of the seven present by the Sea of Tiberias, and he apparently identifies one of these seven with " the disciple whom Jesus loved following " Jesus and Peter (21 : 20), and the claim is pointedly made in 21 : 24 that the disciple whom Jesus loved is the author of the book. If it is not modesty on the part of the author that keeps him from calling himself by name when there was occasion for it, one seems forced to think that the author has a strange prejudice against John the Apostle. One other alternative is, of course, possible, that the writer was trying to create the impression that he was the Apostle John without saying so in plain language. But one who desired to do that would hardly hesitate to go further like the other pseudonymous writings of the period. Delff[1] advocates the view that the author of this Gospel was not one of the Twelve, but a native of Jerusalem and of a family of wealth and priestly rank. There is some attractiveness in this view to Sanday[2] who offers it as a possible alternative to the Johannine authorship which he still tentatively holds. The trouble is that we have to hypothecate an unknown bosom friend of Jesus in Jerusalem outside the number of the Twelve who yet was as close to Jesus as the inner circle of three (Peter, James, and John) in the Synoptic Gospels and who, like John in the Synoptic Gospels and Acts and Galatians, was also a companion of Simon Peter. There is also left unexplained the apparent prejudice against John the Apostle in the Fourth Gospel. The Gospel itself, taken in connection with the facts in the Synoptic Gospels, calls for the Apostle John as the author. Sanday[3] holds that this is " the more natural and obvious view." The arguments for it are very strong as presented by Luthardt,[4] Light-

---

[1] "Das Vierte Evangelium wiedergestellt" (1890); "Neue Beiträge zur Kritik und Erklärung des vierten Evangeliums" (1890).

[2] "The Criticism of the Fourth Gospel," pp. 17, 107. Swete ("The Journal of Theological Studies," July, 1916, pp. 271–278) puts the view of Delff plausibly as a tentative alternative to the Johannine authorship.

[3] "Criticism of the Fourth Gospel," p. 107.

[4] "St. John the Author of the Fourth Gospel" (1875).

foot,[1] Westcott,[2] Ezra Abbott,[3] Godet,[4] Zahn,[5] B. Weiss,[6] Dods,[7] James Drummond,[8] Sanday,[9] Stanton,[10] Watkins.[11] These are weighty names in modern criticism and they offer powerful arguments for the position that the Apostle John wrote the Fourth Gospel. He was a Jew, a Palestinian, and an eye-witness of the ministry of Jesus, and claims the most intimate relation with Jesus. All this points to John beyond a doubt and the argument is to me satisfactory and convincing.

Probably there would have arisen no doubt on the subject if we did not have the Apocalypse of John which expressly claims to have been written by a "John" (Rev. 1 : 9). The tone and temper of this book, along with its grammatical solecisms, have led many to conclude that the same

[1] "Biblical Essays," pp. 1–122.

[2] Vol. I of his commentary (1909), pp. ix–clxxviii.

[3] "Critical Essays" (1888), pp. 9–108.

[4] "Commentary on the Gospel of John," 2 vols. (1886–1890).

[5] "Introduction to the New Testament," 3 vols. (1909).

[6] "A Manual of Introduction to the New Testament," 2 vols. (1889); "Dritte Auflage" (1897). "Meyer-Komm. 9 Aufl." (1902).

[7] "Expositor's Greek Testament" (1902).

[8] "An Inquiry into the Character and Authorship of the Fourth Gospel" (1904).

[9] "The Criticism of the Fourth Gospel" (1905).

[10] "The Gospels as Historical Documents," Part I (1903).

[11] "Modern Criticism Considered in Relation to the Fourth Gospel" (1890).

man cannot be the author of both books. The Epistles cause little difficulty since in style they closely resemble the Gospel. There are, to be sure, men who deny the real Johannine authorship of any of these books, like Moffatt, who regards the author of the original Fourth Gospel (chaps. 1–20) and the Appendix (chap. 21) as " both unknown " [1] and the author of the Apocalypse as probably the Presbyter John.[2] He admits the possibility that the Presbyter John is the author of all the Johannine writings. Papias, as quoted by Eusebius,[3] is responsible for the theory that the Presbyter John is the author of one or of all the Johannine books. " The elder " (3 John 1) is the author of the Third Epistle of John. But it is by no means certain that Papias means to assert the separate existence of the " Presbyter John." He may simply be repeating his reference to the Disciple or Apostle John.[4] Some, accepting this nebulous " Presbyter John," would claim the Gospel and Epistles for him and the Apocalypse for the Apostle John because of its grammatical crudities (cf. Acts 4 : 13). Others would argue precisely the other way and claim the Gospel for the Apostle and the Apocalypse for the Presbyter.

There is thus a considerable body of opinion

[1] " Introduction to the Literature of the New Testament " (1911), p. 570.

[2] *Ibid.*, p. 615.

[3] Eus. H. E., Vol. III, p. 39, ὁ πρεσβύτερος Ἰωάννης.

[4] See the matter argued by Dom Chapman, " John the Presbyter and the Fourth Gospel " (1911).

against the Johannine authorship of the Fourth
Gospel represented by such names as Bacon, H. J.
Holtzmann, O. Holtzmann, Jülicher, Loisy, Moffatt,
Pfleiderer, Reville, Schmiedel, Wernle, Wrede.
There is obviously not room in my book for an
examination of the various objections raised by
these critics to the Johannine authorship of the
Fourth Gospel. They are presented both on in-
ternal and external grounds and are ably and subtly
argued. In general it may be said that these men
reject the supernatural and the deity of Jesus Christ,
though this is by no means true of Moffatt who
ably defends both positions, and not wholly true of
Bacon. *Per contra*, it is pleasant to note that both
Ezra Abbott and James Drummond are Unitarians
and no writers have produced abler defenses of the
Johannine authorship than they have done. Bishop
Lightfoot[1] once said that the opponents of the
Johannine authorship of the Fourth Gospel were
either Rationalists who rejected the supernatural or
Unitarians who denied the deity of Christ Jesus.
This is not precisely true to-day as Bacon[2] shows,
although it is to some extent. Bacon himself is a
keen representative of those who wish to hold on
in some form to belief in the deity of Jesus and yet
who find themselves much puzzled by modern
knowledge in science and Biblical criticism.[3] He
overemphasizes the contrast between the Fourth

---

[1] " Biblical Essays," p. 47.
[2] " The Fourth Gospel in Research and Debate " (1910),
pp. 2 f.   [3] *Ibid.*, pp. 535 f.

Gospel and the Synoptic Gospels and bluntly says that both accounts cannot be true and we must make our choice.[1] This standpoint is only true of those who hang up on this or that detail and lose a clear grasp of the total picture. No one has put the case against the Johannine authorship more adroitly than has Bacon, though his objections are in the main those of his predecessors. The style of the narrative and of the discourses is the same; the picture of Jesus differs radically from that of the Synoptics; the teaching of Jesus in language and thought is too unlike that of the Synoptics; the philosophy of the book is Alexandrian (like Philo); the book is a later development of Hellenism and Paulinism and even with Gnostic tendencies; the language is too finished for John the fisherman-apostle. These arguments are more or less impressive, but are all capable of a different shading in entire harmony with the Johannine authorship. If John lived to the close of Domitian's reign, as Irenæus says he did, he had ample opportunity in Ephesus for contact with Hellenistic, Gnostic, and Philonic teaching and for the furbishing of his style, if indeed a group of friends there did not read the manuscript for him. Contrast the " we" and the " I" in 21 : 24, 25. An old man would naturally tend to report the dialogue somewhat in his own style. Indeed, the Synoptic Gospels vary greatly in the report of the words of Jesus, some of which

[1] " The Fourth Gospel in Research and Debate " (1910), pp. 3 f.

certainly were translated from the Aramaic. It would not be surprising if Paul had some influence on John the Apostle as he did upon Simon Peter. It is not true that the picture of Jesus in the Fourth Gospel differs wholly from that in the Synoptic Gospels nor even from that in Q (the Logia of Jesus) supposed to lie behind our present Matthew and Luke. In Q Jesus is both Lord and Christ and makes claims to a rank above that of man.

There are other theories about the Gospel of John. Some men admit a Johannine kernel and explain the book as the work of a disciple of the Apostle John or as the work of a Johannine school. These views are held in various forms by von Dobschütz,[1] Harnack,[2] Briggs,[3] Wendt.[4] Sanday[5] considers all these efforts " foredoomed to failure " and I agree with him. Some of these theories also suggest a great deal of transposition of material which is a rather easy way out of a difficulty.

This great problem will continue to be discussed and men will be convinced one way or the other partly by temperament and predisposition. There is no such thing as absolute impartiality. It would probably be wholly negative and ineffective if it

[1] " Probleme des apostolischen Zeitalters " (1904).

[2] " Chronologie d. altchristlichen Litteratur."

[3] " General Introduction to Scriptures " (1899); " New Light on the Life of Jesus " (1904).

[4] " The Teaching of Jesus " (1892); " The Gospel According to John : An Inquiry into its Genesis and Historical Value " (1892).

[5] " Criticism of the Fourth Gospel," p. 22.

were found. I have not space here to give the
reasons for the faith that is in me for the Johannine
authorship of the Fourth Gospel, but I at least may
be allowed to say that the reasons are satisfying to
my own mind after due and long consideration of
the minute and zealous criticism on all sides of the
problem. There is one point at least that I wish to
accent a bit, and that is the double strain in John's
own temperament. Jesus called John and James
Boanerges, or sons of thunder (Mark 3 : 17), and
the selfish ambition of these two men and their
mother when they requested the two best places in
the temporal kingdom (Matt. 20 : 20; Luke 18 : 35)
which they expected justifies this description. Besides, they wished to call down fire on the Samaritan
village that did not welcome Jesus. John wished
to stop a man who was casting out demons in the
name of Jesus, but who did not belong to the company of the Twelve (Mark 9 : 38 f. ; Luke 9 : 49 f.).
And yet if John was the author of the Fourth
Gospel and the disciple whom Jesus loved, a wonderful change must have come over him. That is
possible. I happen to know that Basil Manly, Jr.,
who used to be called " the Beloved John " because
of his gentleness and grace, was once a man of
violent temper with occasional outbursts of vehemence. But he overcame his temper. However, in
the First Epistle of John we still see both traits in
the old disciple who writes so tenderly to the " little
children " about love (1 John 2 : 7–17) and almost
in the same breath says that the man is " a liar "

who claims to know God and does not keep His
commandments (1 John 2 : 4). There is the crash
of the thunderbolt still and the lightning flash of
anger in the old man yet as he rages against the
professional pietists who claimed exclusive mystic
knowledge of God but denied Him by their loose
living, justifying themselves by their Gnostic philosophy. The Apocalypse has still more of the thunder and the lightning, but even here there are
flashes of tenderness and notes of love and grace.

I may be allowed to say in passing that, while
the Apocalypse presents difficulties all its own, it is
entirely possible that the linguistic freedom seen
there may be partly due to the excitement of the
visions and partly to lack of revision owing to the
author's isolation on the Isle of Patmos.[1] The language in John 21 : 24 may suggest that the Ephesian elders revised the work of the Apostle. But
this matter is not an essential phase of the problem
of the Fourth Gospel. We must not forget how
much we do not know of the work and growth of
the Apostle John, who had no Luke to record his
deeds for future ages after the opening chapters of
Acts, and even there John is distinctly overshad-
owed by Simon Peter. The figure of the Apostle
John remains in the shadow, now behind Jesus, now
behind Peter, and now behind Paul. And yet this
quiet (anon explosive) man of poetic and reflective
temperament outlived all the circle of the Twelve.

[1] See Robertson, " Grammar of the Greek New Testament in the Light of Historical Research," pp. 133–137.

It was his glory to be the eagle of that circle and to fly higher than any of them in his flight after the truth that is in Jesus. He became the Mystic Christian[1] who rivalled " Paul the Mystic."[2] His old age is delicately alluded to in the Epilogue to his Gospel (John 21 : 20–23) and the misapprehension of the word of Jesus about it corrected.[3] But John lived through the entire wonderful first century A. D. He knew the humble life around the Sea of Galilee and followed Jesus till Calvary came and the Resurrection and the Ascension. He was at Pentecost and shared the prison with Peter during the early years in Jerusalem. He was co-labourer with Peter, James and Paul (Gal. 2 : 1–10) in the great missionary plans for the age. Canon Selwyn (*The Expositor*, September, 1916, pp. 229–236) claims that in John 3: 32–35 John makes a direct reference to Ephesians 4 : 16. If true, there is certainly no harm in it and no surprise about it, for these are probably the writer's own words. He is said to have lived long in Ephesus after Jerusalem was destroyed and the Temple gone. He lived on after the men of the first age of Christianity had disappeared. He was able to look back upon the old Judaism and the early Christianity and upon the later expansion into a world faith in competi-

---

[1] Cf. Watson, " The Mysticism of St. John's Gospel " (1916).   [2] Campbell, 1907.
[3] I wish to call especial attention to the beautiful sketch of the life of John the Apostle in Stalker's " The Two Johns " (1895). ·

tion with the cults of the East and the philosophies
of Greece in the great new age of Roman imperial-
ism. And John seeks to interpret Jesus after many
others had done it with great ability and success,
and yet he carried within his breast hallowed memories of hours on the bosom of Christ, a rich legacy
of words that he must tell before he die.

2. The Purpose.

The author tells us himself why he writes his
Gospel: " Many other signs therefore did Jesus in
the presence of the disciples, which are not written
in this book: but these are written that ye may
believe that Jesus is the Christ, the Son of God;
and that believing ye may have life in his name"
(John 20: 30 f.). His purpose[1] is thus avowedly
stated to be to induce continued[2] belief that the
man Jesus, whose career he has portrayed in part,
is the Anointed One,[3] the Hebrew Messiah of promise and hope, and also the Son of God[4] (not a son
of God, but the Only-begotten Son of God as he
has previously shown); and last, but not least, his
further purpose is that thus the readers of the book
may by believing[5] have life[6] in the name[7] of Jesus.
The author is thus perfectly frank with his readers.

---

[1] Note ἵνα in the full final sense.
[2] Linear tense πιστεύητε (present subjunctive).
[3] ὁ χριστός.   [4] ὁ υἱὸς τοῦ θεοῦ.   [5] πιστεύοντες.
[6] ζωὴν ἔχητε. Keep on having life.
[7] ἐν τῷ ὀνόματι. Name here stands for the power of Jesus
as in the Old Testament usage and this usage occurs also in
the papyri.

He is a preacher first of all of life by faith in Jesus
Christ, the Son of God.   He is in no wise ashamed
of that fact.   He is, besides, an apologist for Christianity.   He has laid down a thesis in the Prologue
of the Gospel to the effect that the Logos or Word,
the Eternal Son of God (1 : 1, 18), was not only with
God in the Pre-incarnate state, but was also God;
and that this Logos, who was God, became flesh
and dwelt among men (1 : 14), who beheld His
glory and testified to His power.   This thesis he
sets out to prove.   He claims that he has succeeded
in his undertaking and hopes to win converts to
Christ by his book.

There are critics who say at once that this is
history with a purpose and hence it is devoid of
real historical value.   But this is very superficial
criticism at best and implies that historians write
in a purely objective way like the Anglo-Saxon
Chronicle.   This is, of course, untrue.   No history
worth the reading is other than the writer's interpretation and arrangement of the facts to prove his
philosophy of history.   This is just as true of
Ferrero's " Greatness and Decline of Rome " as of
Gibbon's " Decline and Fall of the Roman Empire."
Purely objective historical writing is a myth in so
far as it applies to the interpreters of men and
movements of the ages.   Moffatt,[1] though not accepting the Johannine authorship, pointedly says :
" The day is now over, or almost over, when the

[1] " Introduction to the Literature of the New Testament,"
p. 540.

Fourth Gospel and the Synoptists could be played off against each other in a series of rigid antitheses, as though the one were a matter-of-fact and homogeneous chronicle and the other a spiritual reading of the earlier tradition. The problem is too delicate and complex for such crude methods. Recent criticism of the Synoptic Gospels has brought them nearer to the Fourth Gospel." The Gospel of Matthew is just as much a treatise as is the Gospel of John. The one undertakes to show that Jesus of Nazareth is the Messiah of the Jews, the other to prove that He is the Son of God. And Mark's Gospel is really a pamphlet to set forth the power of God in the work of Christ with the necessary implications and inferences of a theological nature concerning the person and claims of Jesus. Luke, the Hellenistic historian, with the scholar's instincts and habits (Luke 1 : 1–4), though expressly claiming to write accurately, by no means presents a colourless narrative, for he clearly takes sides in the issue about Jesus whose deeds and teachings he sets forth in the Gospel and also in the Acts (Acts 1 : 1–5). The New Testament writers are all advocates of Jesus as the Christ, the Son of God, else they would not have written at all. It is preposterous to say that the very men who knew most by personal experience and by research about Jesus were the least qualified to set forth a true record of His character and worth. There is in them the bias of love, but not the blindness of love. Indeed, nothing is more striking in all the Gospels than the naïve truthfulness in the report of the dullness of these very men in the presence of the full brightness of Christ's glory.   The Gospels are, to be sure, to be studied like other historical documents, but certainly with the same spirit of fairness that is accorded to Thucydides and Livy (which is by no means always the case).   There is also the additional circumstance of the greatness of the character who is here set forth.   This latter point is not reasoning in a circle, for the Gospels did not create Jesus Christ.   To be sure He began His career as Jesus and won the title of the Christ, but it is not true that early Christianity is merely the record of the deification of Jesus.   There was a " Jesus or Christ " controversy,[1] but it was fought before a pen was

[1]For modern "Jesus or Christ" controversy see the *Hibbert Journal Supplement* (Reprint for January, 1909); Abbott, "The Son of Man" (1910); Bacon, "Jesus the Son of God" (1911); Briggs, "The Incarnation of Our Lord" (1902); Bruce, "The Humiliation of Our Lord" (1902); Denney, "Jesus and the Gospel" (1908); Dorner, "History of the Development of the Doctrine of the Person of Christ," (5 vols., 1878); Fairbairn, "The Place of Christ in Modern Theology" (1893); Feine, "Jesus Christus und Paulus" (1905); Forrest, "The Christ of History and Experience" (1897), "The Authority of Christ" (1906); Forsyth, "The Person and Place of Jesus Christ" (1909); Gifford, "The Incarnation" (1897); Gore, "The Incarnation of the Son of God" (1891); Knowling, "Testimony of St. Paul to Christ" (2d edition, 1911); Liddon, "Our Lord's Divinity" (1889); Mackintosh, "The Doctrine of the Person of Jesus Christ" (1912); A. Meyer, "Jesus or Paul" (1909); Nicoll, "The Church's One Foundation" (1902); Parker, "Ecce Deus" (1875); Sanday, "Chris-

put to paper and the record of it is told in the Gospels themselves. Here we see how the claims of Jesus were met, how the little band of believers were true when the ecclesiastics closed round the Master in hate, how they fell away in sheer despair when He lay buried in Joseph's tomb, how they won their way back to faith and hope in the Risen Lord by His own triumph over their stubborn doubts, how at last power came after the Risen Lord ascended on high with the promise to return and with the enlightenment of the Holy Spirit to help them interpret the wondrous Being whom they had known. All this is clearly set forth in all the Gospels and in the opening chapters of Acts. These men grew, to be sure, in the fullness of their knowledge of the significance of Jesus, as He had promised that they should under the tutelage of the Holy Spirit (John 15:26; 16:14). The same story is repeated in the growth of Paul as is told in the Acts and in his Epistles. But no one of these men grew more than did the gifted son of Zebedee, who in spite of lack of the culture of the schools, like Bunyan, had the spark of genius and the supreme culture of the spirit through suffering and long reflection and communion with God. " The

tologies Ancient and Modern " (1910); Schweitzer, " The Quest of the Historical Jesus " (1910); Stalker, " The Christology of Jesus " (1901); Thorburn, " Jesus the Christ : Historical or Mythical " (1912) ; Warfield, " The Lord of Glory " (1907); Weinel, " Jesus im neunzehnten Jahrhundert " (1906); J. Weiss, " Christ : The Beginnings of Dogma " (1911).

Historical Value of the Fourth Gospel" is the title of an excellent volume[1] that seeks to sift and weigh the various portions of the story of Jesus as told in John's "*Memorabilia*" of a greater than Socrates and by a greater than Xenophon or Plato. But just as we can get a true picture of Socrates from both Xenophon and Plato who differ greatly in style, so we can see Jesus in each and in all the Gospels.

Certain it is that to-day scholars are much more inclined to credit historical statements in the Fourth Gospel when standing alone than was once the case.[2] The danger of our deciding what could or could not have taken place in ancient days is a

[1] By E. H. Askwith, 1910. E. F. Scott ("The Historical and Religious Value of the Fourth Gospel," 1909) thinks (p. 83) that John "has modified and idealized the facts," but yet "it possesses an inestimable value even for history."

[2] After I had written this portion of my discussion I read with much interest in the September *Expositor* (1916) Rev. John Macaskill's article on "A Transformation in Socratic Criticism—with an Analogy." Here the strong defense of the correctness of Plato's presentation of Socrates by Prof. John Burnet in his "Greek Philosophy" is deftly used by the writer as a parallel to the Fourth Gospel. The Synoptics are more like Xenophon and the Fourth Gospel like Plato. Professor Burnet takes Plato as the true interpreter of Socrates instead of Xenophon, contrary to the usual custom. Macaskill argues cleverly that Socrates may be correctly presented by both writers, Socrates in different moods. "As it was reserved to Plato with his metaphysical insight to give to the world the higher flights of his master's genius, so it may have been reserved to some 'beloved disciple' to interpret the larger and the diviner elements in the teaching of Jesus."

perilous proceeding as Inge [1] so well shows. At
best we have only fragments of the life and teachings of Jesus as John himself says (21 : 25) in a
beautiful hyperbole, if you will, but which clearly
recognizes the partial nature of the book of John.
Indeed, if John seems to have caught one strain in
the music of Christ's life to the exclusion of other
notes, that in itself is not inconceivable on the part
of the bosom friend of Jesus whose sensitive nature
responded best to that high key. But it is more
than curious that the *logion* in Matthew 11 : 27
(Luke 10 : 21) is in precisely the style of the discourses of Jesus in John ; and this *logion* goes back
to the Q of criticism. The very claim to intimate
fellowship with Jesus on the part of the author pre-
pares one to expect in the Fourth Gospel an un-
usual amount of original material as the justification
for a later book in addition to the three well-known
and long accepted Synoptic Gospels. The book is
not to be discounted because of the personality of
the writer, but is to be interpreted in the light of
it. There is, no doubt, some shading by that rich
personality through the mellow mist of the long
years since the now old man mingled so freely in the
years of his youth with the incomparable Person
whose light even now dazzles John as he writes.
But John has truthfully drawn the Portrait of Christ
as he saw Him, and as He is, a picture that in a
wonderful way supplements and harmonizes with

[1] " The Historical Value of the Fourth Gospel " (" Cambridge Biblical Essays," 1909).

that drawn in the Synoptic Gospels. Neither is a
complete picture of the Christ nor both combined.
My purpose therefore is frankly not to find fault
with John for the way in which he has presented
the story of Jesus, but to interpret that story, so
far as I may, for those who wish to follow John as
guide. E. F. Scott (" The Fourth Gospel ; Its Purpose and Theology," 1906, p. 15) says : " Ignorant
as we are of the personality of the writer, we are
forever deprived of the ultimate key to his Gospel."
But I do not believe that we are so ignorant and
the writer gives us the key himself. If John the
Apostle did not write the book, we have to imagine
an unknown genius equal to the task.

3. The Method.

The writer in the Epilogue (21 : 25) tells us that
" there are also many other things which Jesus did,
the which if they should be written every one, I
suppose that even the world itself would not contain
the books that should be written." The " many
others," [1] are of a similar nature. John has made a
brief selection out of a great mass of material. He
has " sampled " the deeds and words of Jesus without any attempt to be exhaustive. This, of course,
he had a perfect right to do. This, in fact, is what
all historians and biographers do. They pick out
and arrange and expound in order to throw a true
picture on the pages which they write. The same
method appears in the Synoptic Gospels which often

[1] ἄλλα, not ἕτερα.

speak of the great number of miracles which Jesus did without any effort to give details.[1] But John spoke also of the embarrassment of the wealth of material at his disposal in 20: 30: " Many other signs therefore did Jesus in the presence of his disciples, which are not written in this book." Here we have two additional statements. One is that he speaks of " signs." [2] He in this book is regarding the works of Jesus as " signs " or " proofs " (cf. " many proofs " [3] in Acts 1 : 3) of the claims of Jesus to be the Son of God. The other point is that these other " signs " were also wrought " in the presence of the disciples," " in the eye of " [4] the " learners " [5] who sat at the feet of the greatest teacher of the ages. John is fully conscious that he has not produced all the proof that is at hand, evidence from eye-witnesses [6] who saw the " signs " and heard the words of Jesus. Some of these were still living when John wrote, as many were still alive who had seen the Risen Jesus when Paul wrote to the Corinthians (1 Cor. 15 : 6). John has obviously made a selection of a few of the " signs " that suited his purpose best. " But these are written, that ye may believe that Jesus is the Christ, the Son of God; and that believing ye may have life in his

---

[1] Cf. Matthew 4 : 23–25; Mark 1 : 35–39; Luke 4 : 42–44.

[2] $\sigma\eta\mu\epsilon\hat{\iota}o\nu$ instead of $\tau\acute{\epsilon}\rho\alpha\varsigma$ (wonder, *miraculum*, miracle) or $\delta\acute{\upsilon}\nu\alpha\mu\iota\varsigma$ (power, dynamite). It requires all these words adequately to describe a gospel miracle. Cf. Acts 2 : 22.

[3] $\dot{\epsilon}\nu$ $\pi o\lambda\lambda o\hat{\iota}\varsigma$ $\tau\epsilon\kappa\mu\eta\rho\acute{\iota}o\iota\varsigma$.   [4] $\dot{\epsilon}\nu\acute{\omega}\pi\iota o\nu$.

[5] $\mu\alpha\theta\eta\tau\hat{\omega}\nu$.   [6] $\alpha\dot{\upsilon}\tau\acute{o}\pi\tau\alpha\iota$ (Luke 1 : 2).

name " (John 20 : 31). Here John has laid bare
his plan with the utmost frankness. If we turn
back and go over the whole Gospel, we shall find
that he has correctly described his work. Chapter 1
is an introductory picture of the Eternal Logos, the
Witness of the Baptist, and the First Disciples, but
the First Miracle or " sign " comes in 2 : 1–11. In
2 : 13–22 there is a demand for a " sign " in proof
of the Messianic prerogatives assumed by Jesus in
the Temple. This incident leads to the case of
Nicodemus in chapter 3. Chapter 4 gives a miracle of grace in the conversion of the Samaritan
woman greater than the healing of the nobleman's
son at Capernaum at the close of it. Chapter 5 is
a picture of the miracle by the Pool of Bethesda in
Jerusalem and the controversy over it. Chapter 6
tells of the miracle of Feeding the Five Thousand
near Bethsaida-Julias and the controversy in the
synagogue in Capernaum that grew out of it. In
chapters 7 and 8 we have an echo of the miracle at
Jerusalem in chapter 5 and chapter 9 sets forth with
great detail the case of the man born blind which
runs in its results into chapter 10. Chapter 11 is
the great miracle of the Raising of Lazarus with its
effect on the Sanhedrin. The result of these and
other deeds of Jesus leads to the climax in Jerusalem. Chapter 12 gives a private and a public
glimpse of Jesus just before the end. Chapters
13–17 are the most distinctive thing in the Gospel,
the Heart of Christ, as He unfolds to the eleven the
inner secrets of His soul. John shortens the de-

tails about the Trial and Crucifixion (chaps. 18 and 19) and adds fresh items of his own. Likewise the appearances in chapters 20 and 21 are from a fresh angle. Chapter 21 centers round the miracle of the fishes.

But John does not merely relate fresh miracles; he has only eight in all. He uses the narrative of the selected miracles as turning-points in his story and connects the discourses with them. In other words, he chooses a very small number of " signs " which illustrate the power of Jesus from various angles and interprets their bearing on the work and mission of Christ both from his own standpoint and in their effect on friend and foe. The signs are hinges in the narrative.

In his use of dialogue John gives a dramatic effect to his book. Indeed, the Gospel of John is as dramatic in effect as the Book of Job and requires the most careful reading and comprehension of the various parts if one is to understand what seems at first so simple. He has a marvellous clarity and simplicity in the use of words which deceives one into thinking that one understands the book without much thinking. But, if he loves to use a comparatively few and more or less common words [1] to express his ideas, let no one imagine that there is a paucity of ideas or any shallowness of thought be. cause of that fact. There is consummate art in the author's use of parallelism and antithesis, repetition and delicate turns of language. There is no arti-

[1] Cf. Abbott, " Johannine Vocabulary " (1905); " Johannine Grammar " (1906).

ficiality, but the very pulsing of life. Few men
have ever written more realistic lines than can be
found in chapters 7–11 where the tension is at the
highest point. It is not always clear when the author is giving the thought of Jesus and when his
own as in 3 : 16–21, 31–36.

The most striking thing about the material in
the Gospel is, not simply that it is nearly all additional to what we have in the Synoptic Gospels,
but also that the gaps in the narrative are so wide
apart. The opening chapters fill out in brief outline
an early ministry of a year's duration previous to
the great Galilean ministry of the Synoptics. There
may be a year between chapters 5 and 6 and six
months between chapters 6 and 7. There are apparently some three months between verses 21 and
22 of chapter 10. John also mentions three passovers (2 : 23; 6 : 4; 12 : 1) and a fourth is possible
(5 : 1). He gives chiefly the Jerusalem ministry as
the Synoptics tell mainly of the Galilean work. It is
obvious that the author is familiar with the Synoptic
Gospels and selects his material chiefly from the great
mass outside of their narratives, but with no hostile
purpose at all. He was in a position, as the Beloved
Disciple, to do a unique service for his Master and he
does it with supreme genius and consummate skill.

One must not forget that, when John wrote
towards the close of the first century A. D., he is no
longer the young man that he was when first he
saw Jesus and followed Him (John 1 : 37). He must
inevitably look back upon the treasured words and

deeds of Jesus out of a rich and long experience.
He had tested the life that is in Christ in his own
heart and in the lives of many others. He himself
has grown tremendously with the years. He is
now John the Theologian.[1] He is a citizen of the
great world and looks at Christianity more from the
world-view from Ephesus and is able to speak of
" the Jews " as if he were not one himself, for now
the Jews and the Christians are separate. But if
John is now cosmopolitan with a touch of Philo or
even of Plato in his intellectual equipment, he is
still more a citizen of heaven. The story may or
may not be true that John ran out of the public
bath when Cerinthus came in for fear that harm
might come to him in the presence of the great
Gnostic heretic. He was still the Son of Thunder.

It may be true that he used to say, " Little children, love one another," as he was borne about in his
chair in his old age. But it is true that John felt himself a citizen of heaven in as true a sense as Paul did
and surpassed Paul in the steadiness of his gaze into
the eternal mysteries of grace in Christ Jesus Paul
has more heat and a stronger blaze, but John has more
light for those with eyes to see into the depths with
him. Watson's closing chapter in his " Mysticism
of St. John's Gospel " is " The Practical Application
of the Incarnation." That is John's idea. He is
no idle " crystal gazer." He is a practical mystic,
" that believing ye may have life in his name." He
is sure that Jesus is Life and can give life.

[1] ὁ θεολόγος.

II

THE MANIFESTATION OF THE MESSIAH

(Chapters 1–4)

" *We have found the Messiah.*"

1. The Prologue (1 : 1–18).

VOLUMES[1] have been written upon these verses alone for they challenge attention by the very boldness of the language used and as a forecast of the thought of the entire book. Many continue to be puzzled as well as charmed by this remarkable picture of the eternal relations of the Son of God. The other Gospels have shown Jesus to be the Saviour, the Messiah, the Son of man, and the Son of God. In Matthew and in Luke the nature of Jesus Christ is shown to be both divine and human since He is begotten of the Virgin Mary by the Holy Spirit (Luke 1 : 26–38 ; Matt. 1 : 18–25). Jesus is presented as sinless and well-pleasing to His Father. But John treats the Incarnation as only an incident in the life of the Son of God. He is profoundly convinced both of the humanity and the deity of Jesus Christ. He insists against the Docetic Gnostics that Jesus shed real blood on

[1] Cf. Baldensperger's " Der Prolog des vierten Evangeliums " (1898) ; Harnack, " Ueber das Verhältniss des Prologs des vierten Evangeliums zum ganzen Werke " (1892).

34

the Cross of which he was a personal witness (John 19 : 35). But he is equally confident against the Cerinthian Gnostics that Jesus and the Christ are one and the same person, Son of man and Son of God. He will have none of the notion that the Æon Christ came on Jesus at His baptism and left Him at His death. The Word became flesh (1 : 14), but retained the same personality. As Christianity came into contact with rival faiths, it was inevitable that Christian leaders and teachers should reëxamine their theology in the new outlook as they had done in the light of Judaism. Comparative religion was not an academic procedure for Paul as it is not to-day for the wide-awake missionary in China, India, or Japan where one has to expound his faith in terms intelligible to followers of Buddha or Confucius. Paul quickly took the language of the Stoics and of the Mystery-religions [1] of the day (Mithraism and the rest), but without adopting their ideas or standpoint. He filled their language which they understood so well with the rich content of Christian truth. It is not a bit surprising to find the Apostle John doing the same thing. We know now that the Jewish Palestinian theology of the first century A. D. was a richer thing than was once supposed to be true. Hellenism was married to Judaism in Alexandria, but in Palestine itself not all the Jews followed blindly the scribes in the letter of the law. There was an appreciable body of intelligent

[1] Cf. Kennedy, "St. Paul and the Mystery-Religions" (1913).

opinion represented by the Apocalyptists (as in the Testaments of the Twelve Patriarchs, the Book of Enoch, etc.) that sought the spirit rather than the letter and hungered for a higher type of Messiah than the average Pharisaic rabbi of the period.[1] But the disciples of Christ came to see that Christ was higher and richer in His nature and work than was outlined in the Old Testament Scriptures. Paul himself plainly sets forth the cosmic relations of Jesus Christ in Colossians 1 : 15–17. The writer of Hebrews does the same thing in Hebrews 1 : 1–3 in language redolent of the Alexandrian philosophy. Jesus as the Son of God did sustain relations to the universe, and the Christians early came to see it. Jesus had claimed this power while on earth (cf. Matt. 28 : 18). Already Philo in Alexandria had taken over the Stoic doctrine of the Logos as both Reason and Word and had made abundant use of it. The same usage had occurred before him in the so-called Wisdom of Solomon. Indeed, the Targums made free use of the *Mêmra* (word) as the personification of God. The personification of Wisdom is common in the wisdom books of the Old Testament as in Proverbs 8 : 22–30. Indeed, Prof. J. Rendel Harris[2] argues that, since Paul calls Jesus " The Wisdom of God and the Power of God"

---

[1] Cf. Charles, " Religious Development between the Old and the New Testaments " (1914) ; Oesterley, " Doctrinal Teaching of the Apocrypha " (1914).

[2] In *The Expositor* for August, September, etc., 1916, " The Origin of the Prologue to St. John's Gospel."

(1 Cor. 1 : 31) and since in Luke 11 : 49 the Wisdom of God is personified, we need not be surprised at John's use of the term Logos. In fact, he argues very plausibly that the use of Wisdom in Proverbs 8 : 22–30 was what suggested John's use of Logos in John 1 : 1–18 : " The Lord possessed me (*sophia*) *in the beginning* of his way, before his works of old. I was set up from everlasting, *from the beginning* . . . when he prepared the heavens *I was there :* when he set a compass upon the face of the deep . . . then *I was by him*." One need not follow Professor Harris in all his ingenious suggestions [1] to see that there is a general parallel of thought about Wisdom. In Ephesus, where John probably wrote, the work of the Stoic philosopher Heracleitus was well known. Moffatt [2] even suggests that a Stoic might very well have written : " In the beginning was the Logos, and the Logos was God." Certainly there is no harm in the world in thinking that the aged Apostle, all alert for the thought of his day among educated men, was only too glad to use this Jewish-Platonic-Stoic term Logos as a further effort to expound the nature and mission of Jesus in the universe. It is " an intellectual form " [3]

---

[1] He shows also (*The Expositor*, September, 1916, pp. 166, 169) that Cyprian in his *Testimonia* not only calls Christ the Wisdom and the Word of God, but explains Wisdom as being the Son.

[2] " Introduction to the Literature of the New Testament," p. 525.

[3] Scott, " Historical and Religious Value of the Fourth Gospel," p. 40.

of the Græco-Roman world just as " Messiah " belonged to the Jewish world, but with this difference that the Logos idea was already at home in the Jewish world also. Neither term is a complete presentation of the Person of Christ, but both are useful. It is, however, very difficult to translate Logos into English because of the double idea in it of Reason and Expression. The Poet Laureate, Robert Bridges, translates these words in his new book [1] thus: " In the beginning was mind." That is certainly possible, but it is equally certain that it is not all that John meant by the term as is made plain in 1 : 18 by the words: " he hath declared him." It boots little therefore to try to find the " sources " of the Logos idea so far as John's Prologue is concerned save as an historical preparation for John's concept. It is impossible to fit John's Logos into that of Philo, of Plato, or of Heracleitus, though beyond a doubt traces of each may be found in John's use besides the term given to Wisdom in Proverbs 8 : 22–30. The " Doctrine of the Logos " [2] cannot be carried over bodily into John's Prologue for he adds features of his own. John is not so much concerned with the abstract philosophical conceptions, though he does outline a real philosophy of religion in these verses, as he deals with the revelation of the nature of God in Christ the Logos and Son. [3] It

[1] " The Spirit of Man."
[2] Cf. Scott, " The Fourth Gospel : Its Purpose and Theology," pp. 145–175.
[3] Watson, " Mysticism of St. John's Gospel," Chapter II.

is true that John makes no further use of the term
Logos after he leaves the Prologue, but that fact
does not indicate any change of purpose on his
part. In fact the Logos terminology is merely em-
ployed as an aid to John's purpose in the Prologue
to set forth in bold outline the eternal relation of
the Logos and the broad features of the Incarnation.
He has no further use for such philosophical terms
when he proceeds with the body of his book.

It is not difficult to follow the thought in the
Prologue. We have first the personal relations between the Logos and God (verses 1–2). One is
reminded of Genesis by the opening words. Of
course there never was a " beginning " with God or
with the Logos, but we use the term for all that
portion of eternity previous to man's career. We
have to fall back upon Origen's contradictory language that the Son is eternally begotten. Father
implies Son and yet seems logically to antedate Son.
There we have to leave it. But we are more concerned with the phrase " with God " [1] which does
not have the customary Greek preposition [2] meaning " by the side of," but one that means " face to
face," [3] and suggests the most intimate fellowship
as equals. The flat assertion that " the Logos was
God " [4] has probably created more prejudice against
this Gospel than anything else in it. But this is the

---

[1] πρὸς τὸν θεόν.   [2] παρά.

[3] πρός. Cf. Robertson, " Grammar of the Greek New
Testament in Light of Historical Research," p. 625.

[4] Note ἦν, not ἐγένετο.

thesis of the book. The Pre-incarnate state of the
Logos is not simply affirmed, but it is pointedly asserted that He was God in the sense that the Father
is God.[1] He repeats his point before he goes on.
He next affirms that the Logos was the Agent in
creation (verse 3). He is the intermediate[2] Agent.
He says that not only " all,"[3] but every single
thing[4] was made by Him. One recalls in the
Genesis account how God spoke and it was done.
The full power of creative activity is thus claimed
for Jesus on a par with the Father. It is but a
natural step to say in plain words: " In him was
life." The ancient and more probable punctuation
is : " That which hath been made was life in him "
(verse 4). The creative work of the Word (cf. 5 :
17, " My Father worketh even until now, and I
work") supplied the proof of His being the life of
the world which His personal manifestation in the
Incarnation made plainer (" I am the life," 11 : 25).
John is fond of the words life and light in connection with God (cf. 1 John 1 : 1–7). Indeed, in
1 John 1 : 1 he speaks of " the Word of life " com-
bining the Logos with Life. In Revelation 19 : 13
we find: " And his name is called the Word of
God." Thus the use of the Word as applied to
Jesus is one of the indications of identical authorship for these books. The Gnostics made frequent
mystical use of these terms as did the Mithraists
and other followers of the mystery-religions, but

---

[1] By the use of θεός.   [2] διά.

[3] πάντα.   [4] οὐδὲ ἕν.

John is not afraid to take great words that were
familiar to men and pour into them the truth of
Christ. The term is not unknown in the Psalms
also as applied to God. John's style here is not
simply a mixing of images when he says: " And
the life was the light of men." This is a good
specimen of John's style. He leaves us to relate
the various facts stated. " He is the Light through
the medium of Life " (Westcott, *in loco*). We are
familiar with the properties of radium and elec-
tricity. But no physical image can fully present
the truth about the preëxistent state and work of
the Logos, God's Son. These verses (1–5) are very
wonderful and rich. The Logos was the Light of
men as a whole [1] and not merely the Light of the
Jews. John means, of course, that the Word was
the moral and spiritual Light of all men, all the
real light that they had. Verse 5 pictures the inevitable conflict between light and darkness. It is
the mission of light to drive away darkness. This
is a parable of the eternal conflict between good
and evil, between Christ and Satan. The Temptations of Jesus by Satan are one illustration of it, but
it continues through the ages and we are all sharers
in the struggle (cf. 1 John 1) and must take sides.
We see this conflict in every city and in every ham-
let, in politics, in business, in religion, in school, in
the home, and in every heart. The light shines on
in the darkness, is not discouraged by the long
night and the stubborn and thick darkness. The

[1] τῶν ἀνθρώπων. The article for class.

light will win in the end. " And the darkness overcame it not." This is beyond a doubt the true ren-
dering.[1] We have the same idea in John 12 : 35,
" that darkness overtake you not." [2] John claims
final victory for Christ in Revelation 11 : 15.

Verses 6–8 tell of the work of the Forerunner, a
God-sent man, a real Apostle [3] from God, sent to
bear witness about the Light, to help men see that
He is the true Light of God, that all men may believe in the Light by means of John's witness. One
may think at first that this was a needless mission,
for surely men can tell light from darkness. But
this is precisely what men cannot do. They have
poor eyes, so used to the darkness, blinded by sin
and selfish passions, that false lights easily lead them
astray and they are not able clearly to distinguish
in the flickering shadows. Satan knows this so well
that he himself poses as an angel of light (2 Cor.
11 :14). Indeed, John the Baptist himself was
taken to be the Light in the very act of telling of
the Light (verse 8). It is small wonder then that
multitudes fall victims to every religious dreamer
who comes along, Buddha or Mahomet, Baha or
Besant, Schlatter or Schweinfurth, Joseph Smith or
Mary Baker Eddy. The light-bearer must be sure
that he bears the Light of Life and that men see
what they ought to see. It will be shown that John
was loyal to the Light.

The coming of the Light into humanity was the

---

[1] οὐ κατέλαβεν. [2] ἵνα—μὴ καταλάβῃ.
[3] ἀπεσταλμένος.

crucial time of history. This great era is broadly
sketched in verses 9–14. The Word was the true
light of every man even before the Incarnation.
The Cosmic Christ John has already set forth above,
but this Light was too dimly perceived to be really
effective for the salvation of men. So the promise
was given of the One who was to come into the
world (John 11 : 27).[1] This is probably the idea in
1 : 9, though the words may refer to " every man
coming into the world." But the presence of the
Logos in the world which He had made revealed a
tragedy (verse 10). " The world knew him not,"
" did not recognize him." [2] He was as much a
stranger to the human world after the Incarnation
as He was before. The Light was blazing in the
darkness and the darkness could not see the Light.
Here we are brought face to face with the difficulty
of God in revealing Himself to men. The imma-
nence of God in nature is as true as His transcend-
ence over nature. But how can the Eternal make
Himself known to sinful men? It is only possible
in terms of personality, for men are persons. But
the Tragedy was enough to break the heart of
Christ as it did in the end, this supreme Tragedy
of the Ages and of the Race. At first it was a
" Hebrew Tragedy " (Conder), for He came unto
His own home[3] which He had made and His own
people[4] did not take Him to their homes and their

---

[1] ὁ εἰς τὸν κόσμον ἐρχόμενος. Cf. also John 6 : 14.

[2] αὐτὸν σὺκ ἔγνω.

[3] εἰς τὰ ἴδια.   [4] οἱ ἴδιοι.

hearts,[1] but received Him as a stranger. There
were some who did open their hearts to Him. To
these He gave the right (and the power [2]) to become
the spiritual, not merely the cosmic, children of
God, to those who believe on His name. Thus He
made faith in Himself the touchstone to member-
ship in the family of God. This second birth is of
God. But the cardinal historical fact is that "the
Word became [3] flesh, and tabernacled [4] among us."
The Virgin Birth is not mentioned, but certainly is
not denied. It is rather, I think, implied by the
very language of John which suggests something
other than ordinary generation. Indeed, it is difficult to conceive of a real Incarnation of God in any
other way than that of the narratives in Matthew
and in Luke. "The eternal and divine Christ
entered into this world not by human generation"
(W. P. Du Bose, "Incarnation," *Constructive Quar-
terly*, September, 1916, p. 438). The wonder and
glory of it all John and the rest will never forget,
for "we beheld his glory, glory as of the only-
begotten from the Father" (cf. Luke 9: 32). He
probably refers to the Transfiguration scene. He
was "full of grace and truth."

The Baptist bore witness also after he saw the
Light, not merely beforehand (verse 15). He put
his witness in paradoxical form: "He that cometh
after me is become before me." He was only after

---

[1] οὐ παρέλαβον.   [2] ἐξουσίαν.   [3] ἐγένετο, not ἦν.
[4] ἐσκήνωσεν. Pitched his tent in human flesh. (Cf. 2 Cor.
5 : 1.)

John in order of time and of manifestation in human
birth. He was always before John in eternity and
in eminence and He always will be. This John
saw and said.

The plenitude[1] of Christ (cf. the fullness of the
Godhead bodily in Col. 2 : 9) he has already presented, but now he emphasizes the idea that we
Christians all receive some portion of Christ's grace
and truth (verses 16–18). It is " grace for[2] grace,"
new grace to take the place of the old. The word
Law describes the Mosaic system, but Christ has
given us grace and truth, words rich and fresh with
eternal youth and freedom. Grace shows the love
of God and truth the passion for reality. The
writer has said in 1 : 1 that the Word was God, and
in 1 : 14 that the Word became flesh. Now he com-
bines both ideas in the correct text of 1 : 18, " God
Only-begotten."[3] Only the God-man can fully reveal God to man. He is God and He is man and
can and does act as interpreter of God to man.
" He hath declared him." Jesus, the Logos (Reason and Word of God), the Incarnate God, Son of
God and Son of man, hath made the *Interpretation*[4]
of God that man can read. He is God's Living
Speech, the Eternal Idea of God spoken in flesh
and blood that men may see and hear and handle

---

[1] ἐκ τοῦ πληρώματος αὐτοῦ. He probably has in mind
the Gnostic use of *pleroma* for all the attributes of God.

[2] ἀντί.   [3] θεὸς μονογενής.

[4] ἐξηγήσατο. Cf. our *exegesis*. It is the timeless aorist
here.

(1 John 1 : 1) and yet live and obtain eternal life (John 20: 31) by loving God in Christ.

2. The Witness of the Baptist (1 : 19-36).

As has already been stated, it is not the purpose of this book to expound in detail all the Gospel of John, but only those portions pertinent to the Divinity of Christ. As a matter of fact this method deals with the heart of the Gospel, for this is the theme that is central in John's thought and purpose. In the Prologue he had spoken of the Witness of John concerning the Light. Now he proceeds to tell what the witness is (1 : 19). He selects first the striking incident of the visit of the committee of Sadducees (priests and Levites, 1 : 20) appointed by the Sanhedrin at the suggestion of the Pharisees (1 : 24). John is at Bethany beyond Jordan (1 : 28) after the baptism of Jesus when the committee comes. He had previously denounced the Pharisees and Sadducees in severe terms when they followed the multitudes from Judea and Jerusalem in the earlier stages of his ministry (Matt. 3: 7-10). It is a tremendous tribute to his popular power that the Sanhedrin feels called upon after that rebuke to see if after all he makes any Messianic claims for himself. But John the Baptist does not take it as a compliment. He is greatly perturbed in spirit that any one should so mistake his spirit and message as to imagine that he is capable of such treachery to his Chief. His disclaimer is vehement and repeated. He is not the Christ nor Elijah (in flesh and person) nor the prophet promised by Moses (really the Messiah, though some thought not). He is only a voice crying in the wilderness and the darkness of the night. As the Forerunner of the Messiah he has introduced the new order of baptism which really treats the whole nation as heathen and calls them to repentance. " In the midst of you standeth one whom ye know not " (1 : 26) because of your blinded eyes (cf. 1 : 10 f.). Thus John boldly announces the actual arrival of the Messiah the latchet of whose shoes he is unworthy to unloose (1 : 27).

The committee may have returned to Jerusalem with a puzzled state of mind at these wondrous words. On the next day at any rate John identifies the Messiah to those who are with him (1 : 29–34). " Behold, the Lamb of God that taketh away the sins of the world," he cries as he sees Jesus coming to him. This is a call for the people to see the Light. It is argued that the writer has made the Baptist too theological in this saying and too advanced for his circle. But John's theological atmosphere was not that of the Pharisees whom he denounced. He was a man of the hills and of the Old Testament. He was the son of a priest. He was the last and greatest of the old prophets and the first of the new age. He could see the sacrificial side of the servant of Jehovah in Isaiah 53 and he knew the meaning of the Paschal Lamb. So the Baptist groups the central fact in the work of the Messiah, His atoning death as the Paschal Lamb for the sin of the world. He did, but his hearers did not. John went on to explain the purpose of his preaching and his baptism, to manifest the Messiah to Israel. It was not mere spiritual insight and intuition on John's part, for he had the sign of the Holy Spirit in the form of a dove promised, by which sign he was to recognize the Messiah when He came to ask baptism at his hands. He knew Him not, certainly not as the Messiah, till the instinctive recognition when Jesus came to the Jordan, probably not at all, for John and Jesus lived far apart, though kinsmen. He had seen the Messiah and the sign came also and now John stands here to tell the people that yonder Jesus is the Messiah of promise, the Light and the Life, the Son of God. " I have seen, and have borne witness that this is the Son of God " (1 : 34).[1] The testimony of the Baptist to the Deity of Jesus Christ is thus clear and explicit. But John repeated his witness on the day following (1 : 35 f.). He looked on Jesus as He walked and in his emotion could only say : " Behold, the Lamb of God." But he had two disciples with him who heard this repeated testimony. Jesus went His way and John never saw Him again, but he had borne his witness.

3.   The First Group of Disciples (1 : 37–51).

One of these two disciples was Andrew the brother of Simon (1 : 40) and the other was probably

[1] Note the perfect tenses ἑώρακα, καὶ μεμαρτύρηκα. It is John's settled conviction.

John the brother of James, though that inference is not stated by the correct text of 1:41 "findeth first." [1]   We are not to think that Jesus, though God's Only-begotten Son and in reality God Only-begotten, looked to those who saw Him other than man, for His flesh was a veil to conceal His deity (Heb. 10:20) as well as the Image of the Father whom men should see in Christ (Heb. 1:3; John 14:9).   There was no "posing" as God on the part of Jesus, no striking of attitudes and demanding worship from those who came near Him. We need not trouble ourselves over the term "the Son of God" used by the Baptist nor how much that meant to Andrew and John as they went to spend the first of many wonderful days with Jesus (1:39).   We are not told anything that passed between them, but the result spoke for itself.   Andrew could stand it no longer.   "He findeth first his own brother Simon, and saith unto him, We have found the Messiah." [2]   That was a startling message, but Andrew did not stop with that.   He brought Simon to Jesus, face to face with [3] Jesus.   John seems to have brought James also.   The Light is beginning to shine.   Some are coming into the kingdom.

Now Jesus Himself finds Philip who in turn wins

---

[1] πρῶτον, not πρῶτος.

[2] Εὑρήκαμεν τὸν Μεσσίαν.   We need not discuss the content of the term Messiah in Andrew's mouth.   The Jews differed much themselves about it.   Some assigned divine attributes to the Messiah, but only in a vague way.

[3] πρός.

Nathanael (1:43–51). Nathanael is sceptical and cautious. " Can any good thing come out of Nazareth ? " What a chance for a debate and a wrangle! Nathanael is prejudiced against Jesus because of town pride which is as good a ground as many critics of Jesus have to-day. Philip refused to argue the point and drew Nathanael to the fellowship of Jesus. This he could not well refuse. Once there Jesus paid Nathanael the most delicate compliment, for he was a rare spirit, as is often true of the young men and women with doubts and fears. The surprising insight of Jesus completely won Nathanael who threw away his doubts and cried: " Rabbi, thou art the Son of God; thou art the King of Israel " (1:49). He may have heard the words of the Baptist about Jesus (1:34) and now confesses fully both the Messiahship (King of Israel) and the Deity of Jesus. Nathanael is a true Israelite when he reveals this spiritual insight and quickness of apprehension. The heart of Jesus is comforted by Nathanael's words, for a beginning has been made. Six men, probably all from the circle of the Baptist's disciples, have come out boldly for Him as the Messiah the Son of God. But better things are coming. This has been a Bethel to Jesus and like Jacob of old (Gen. 28:12) He sees a vision of the future work of the Kingdom: " Ye shall see the heaven opened, and the angels of God ascending and descending upon the Son of man " (1:51). Jesus here calls Himself the Son of man, a term applied to the Messiah in the Book of Enoch, but

Christ seems to have chosen it Himself, for it makes a Messianic claim in veiled language and thus avoided technical legal difficulties incident to the use of Messiah, as we shall see. Besides, it presents Jesus as the Representative man of the race as He is. It is as the Son of man, the Mediator between God and man, that He is able to be a " Jacob's ladder" for heaven and earth to meet in Him. The heavens are open to Christ Jesus and men draw near to Him and in Christ can look into heaven. Westcott (Vol. I, p. 79) makes a list of the confessions of Christ made by the successive men and women who come under His power in the Gospel of John. The high confession of the Baptist we have seen, and of Andrew, of Philip, of Nathanael, and now we have the claim of Jesus Himself. If one is surprised that Nathanael should use the words " the Son of God," he must recall that the Baptist heard the Father call Jesus " My Beloved Son " at the baptism (Matt. 3 : 17) and Nathanael probably heard the Baptist's testimony (1 : 34) as already stated.

4. The First Display of Power (2 : 1–11).

In the Prologue John in broad outline presents his conception of the eternal Son of God entering humanity as the Expression of God to reveal the Father to men. Then follows the witness of the Baptist to the fact that Jesus is the Son of God. Next comes the discovery of the first band of believers that Jesus is the Messiah, the Son of God as

shown by the words of Andrew, Philip, and Nathanael, and Christ's own claim about Himself. It
is objected by some modern critics that John's
Gospel is unhistorical in this presentation of the
claims of Jesus, since according to the Synoptic
Gospels Jesus conceals the fact that He is the
Messiah, the Son of God, till the latter part of His
ministry and even then warns the disciples not to tell
what they have found out (Matt. 16 : 13–20). But
on closer examination of the Synoptic Gospels one
notes that they give also the early presentation of
Jesus as the Messiah the Son of God. It is seen
in the words of the Father at the baptism of Jesus
(Matt. 3 : 17 ; Mark 1 : 11 ; Luke 3 : 22) and in the
temptation of Jesus (Matt. 4 : 3 ; Luke 4 : 3) and in
various other ways as in the exclamation of the
healed demoniacs, and the growing appreciation of
the disciples and the people. It is, besides, perfectly natural that in the first year of the public
ministry which the Synoptics omit save the baptism
and temptation, when He is recognized as Messiah,
there should be acknowledgment of Jesus as Messiah in the first glow of enthusiasm till it was seen
that the Pharisees were jealous and hostile when
caution made it wise to omit the term Messiah so
as to avoid the technical charge of blasphemy
(cf. John 4 : 1–4 ; Luke 3 : 19 f.). Indeed, the Gospel
of John itself, which gives the early claims and as-
criptions of Messiahship, shows most clearly of all
the avoidance of the term Messiah on the part of
Jesus in this later ministry (John 8–10). Here,

then, this Gospel, supplementing the Synoptics in the early ministry, gives the touch of life which is needed to fill out the story.

Now comes the first display of power on the part of Jesus, already hailed as Messiah and Son of God, to show that He acts like God. The devil had suggested that Jesus turn the stone into bread to prove that He is a Son of God (Luke 4 : 3). But Jesus needed no such proof. He had known this mystery for long, how long we do not know, for He has had clear Messianic consciousness of this peculiar sonship since He was twelve years old (Luke 2 : 51). The mother of Jesus does not need the miracle to convince her of the nature and mission of her wondrous Son. She had carried His secret in her heart all these years (Luke 2 : 19). But the little band of disciples (probably six in all) did need confirmation of their new faith in Jesus as the Messiah of Israel. It was all so new and strange to them. The protest of Jesus to His mother was not an outburst of impatience with her, but a declaration of independence on His part, for His Messianic activity lay outside of her control. He had gladly been subject to her and to Joseph (Luke 2 : 51), but now He must follow the path that His heavenly Father showed in His great task. The language of Jesus probably means : " What does it matter to you and me ? " It is like our " Never mind." [1] But Mary had a woman's and a mother's instincts and saw beneath the form of

---

[1] τί ἐμοὶ καὶ σοί;

the words and bade the servants to follow the
directions of Jesus. It is useless to quibble over
the miracle of turning the water into wine, this first
miracle wrought by Jesus, and a nature miracle at
that. If we have come thus far in John's Gospel
with any kind of sympathy and assent, we can
easily go the whole way. I am assuming that the
readers of my book have made up their minds about
God and Christ and the world. I am not advocat-
ing obscurantism in any sphere, but just the opposite. I may say frankly that I am not antago-
nistic to evolution as a process used by God in the
creation of the universe. I am not sure that the
evolutionary hypothesis has been proved, but I do
not object in the least if it should be. I have no
fear that science will again become materialistic as
it once threatened to do. It is nothing like so
negative and agnostic as it once was. Modern
scientists, barring Haeckel, are becoming decidedly
spiritualistic in outlook and open advocates of the
supremacy of mind over matter. If we really believe that, there is little to bother over further save
questions of fact. If God created and is creating,
why trouble about the present activity of God?
If Jesus is God, why deny to Him the power of
God? What we call a nature miracle differs no
whit from any other save that we are more familiar
with the impact of mind on mind, though we recognize clearly the power of mind over matter in our
own bodies. The Gospel of John represents Jesus
as justifying His miraculous power on the score of

the continuous activity of His Father (John 5 : 17).
The notion of an absentee God who cannot touch
the work of His own hands with His own will for
fear of upsetting His own laws is puerile.   We are
not to think of God as whimsical, but as personal
and as supreme in every realm, supreme even over
the laws of nature which are simply the orderly expression of His own will.   These laws are meant
for our protection and blessing and they are so.
But it is unscientific and unhistorical to say that
God cannot do this or that unless the thing contradicts God's own nature.   For instance, God cannot lie.

This first miracle of power over inanimate nature
at Cana of Galilee " manifested his glory " as it was
meant to do.   It served immediate need, to be sure,
but it " made plain " [1] the glory of Jesus as the Son
of God in accordance with His claims and the faith
of the disciples who " believed on him " afresh and
more deeply because of this surprising display of
creative activity.   Faith was helped by sight.

5.   The First Clash with the Jerusalem Authorities (2 : 12–22).

The first impression that one gets from this vivid
incident in the Temple in Jerusalem is that of the
feeling of Jesus Himself.   The Synoptics give a
similar account at the close of the ministry (Matt.
21 : 12 f. ; Mark 11 : 15–18 ; Luke 19 : 45–48), which
is entirely possible and reasonable as a last protest

[1] ἐφανέρωσεν.

against the desecration of the Temple by the money
traffic allowed by the ecclesiastical grafters. That
story in no way contradicts or makes incredible this
one at the start. Indeed, if the thing could only
happen once, it is easier to understand it at this
juncture, when for the first time Jesus, conscious of
Messianic authority, meets the abuses in His Father's
house. He is doubtless well aware that his words
and deeds mean the assertion of authority over the
Temple worship in opposition to the official ecclesiastics only sufferable in case the usurper should be
the Messiah Himself. Certainly Jesus did not look
to be that as He came in the garb of a labourer
with a whip of cords in His hand. There was, indeed, a strange majesty of mien, that swept all before
Him, but the Jews soon rallied on the outside and
clamoured for a " sign " in proof of His right to do
such deeds (John 2 : 18). Perhaps they meant that,
as He had no " paper " as a token of legal power,
He should give some heavenly attestation since He
claimed a peculiar relation to God. The reply of
Jesus was not understood by foe or friend, but was
remembered in garbled form against Him till His
trial. Jesus is here presented as conscious of His
death which is foreshadowed by this hostile attitude
of the ecclesiastical authorities on this first appearance of the Messiah in Jerusalem. Jesus means
also that His resurrection shall be the final proof of
His claim to be the Messiah the Son of God. It is
clear that this attitude of Jesus is quite other than
that of modern critics who say that Jesus did not

mean to make any issue with the authorities and only gradually came to feel that He was a possible Messiah and did not expect death as a means of redemption from sin. The trouble about that view is that it is opposed by the Synoptic Gospels (and even by Q) as strongly as by the Gospel of John. In the temptation there is presented the shadow of the Cross and that is before the incident in John 2. In the Synoptic Gospels the death of Christ is soon plain in the background. The Gospel of John cannot be understood unless one is willing to see that Jesus from the start sees the path which He is to tread. Nor can the Synoptics properly be made to mean anything else.

6. The Rush of the Crowd (2 : 23–25).

Jesus would not work a " sign " at the demand of the ecclesiastics (cf. His like refusal to the devil), but He did perform a number in Jerusalem which many beheld and, as a result, many " believed " [1] on Him probably as the Messiah, but certainly in a very superficial way, for Jesus distrusted their profession of faith. There were always great crowds of Jews from all sections at the passover (John 2 : 23). There are always many who are caught in the current and borne along with any new popular movement without clearness of ideas or depth of conviction. Fortunately Jesus, as the Son of God, had the power to read aright the hearts of men and so to guard His mission from these effervescent be-

[1] Cf. $\dot{\epsilon}\pi i\sigma\tau\epsilon\upsilon\sigma\alpha\nu$ with $o\dot{\upsilon}\kappa$ $\dot{\epsilon}\pi i\sigma\tau\epsilon\upsilon\epsilon\nu$.

lievers. " He himself knew what was in man," not
only in one man or in these men, but in all men, in
the race.[1] Here we are given an instance of the
knowledge of Jesus as God, no mere mind reading
or telepathy, but the full insight into the human
heart. Missionaries in heathen lands have to guard
constantly against the rush of people after novelty
as well as against the bread and butter brigade
(cf. John 6).

7. The Secrecy of Nicodemus the Pharisee (3 : 1–21).

Nicodemus had likewise noticed the " signs " of
Jesus (3 : 2) and had reflected on the consequences
of these miracles in connection with the teaching
and claims of Jesus. But he was not like the un-
thinking crowd who were swept off of their feet by
John or Jesus or Barcochba or any other new-
comer. He was a scholar, a theologian, a teacher,
a Pharisee, a member of the Sanhedrin, and, as a
man of importance and standing, owed it to himself to proceed with due caution so as to make no
mistake and avoid needless talk among his asso-
ciates. All the city was agog over the Nazarene,
and it was not easy to manage. So he sought a
visit by night to the tent of the new and irregular
rabbi on the hills near Jerusalem. Jesus is thus face
to face with one of the leading scholars of current

---

[1] ἐν τῷ ἀνθρώπῳ. The generic use ἄνθρωπος and the class
use of the article. Mr. E. S. Buchanon reports a Spanish
manuscript as reading : " For He, being God, knew what
men were."

Pharisaism, who is seeking further light concerning the claims and message of Jesus Himself. It is notorious that scholars are the most difficult men to teach because they know so much already. In the case of Nicodemus, he had his own theology concerning the Messiah and the Kingdom of God, and it was clear that Jesus did not fit into his theories, and yet he was fascinated by Jesus. The effort of Jesus is a kindly and gracious way of enabling Nicodemus to understand the new view-point. He sees into the mind of Nicodemus and may have read the Pharisaic books,[1] for He shows always a thorough understanding of the defects of Pharisaic theology and practice. The new birth, which so puzzled Nicodemus, is the door into the real Kingdom of God which is spiritual. Nicodemus is a tragic instance of the preacher or teacher of heavenly things who has no personal experience behind his words and merely repeats logical conclusions or the parrot-like repetition of sentences which he has been taught. Jesus shows him his ignorance of the elements of true religion and opens the door into the purposes of God in heaven, the great theological problems that concern God's redemptive love. The true text in verse 13 mystifies Nicodemus still more, for it says that the Son of man who descended out of heaven (the Incarnation) " is in heaven " even now while he speaks to Him. Jesus also tells Nicodemus of the death of the Son of man, lifted

[1] Cf. Thomson, " Books Which Have Influenced Our Lord."

up like the serpent in the wilderness that any one
may have eternal life by believing on Him (3 : 14 f.).
It is not certain whether verses 16–21 are the words
of Christ to Nicodemus, as is probable, or the re-
flections of the evangelist on the interview.   But, in
either case, it is a clear announcement that Jesus is
the only begotten [1] Son of God, sent into the world
because of God's love to save the world.   There is
nothing in this wonderful " Little Gospel" (John
3 : 16) that Jesus could not have said at this time to
Nicodemus.   It is all involved in what has preceded.
So then the deity of Jesus is presented to Nicodemus, but we are not told how he received it, for his
own querulous doubts were no longer expressed,
but gave way to silence.   Certainly a deep impression was made upon him by Jesus, and he will
later openly champion His cause (John 7 : 50;
19 : 39), though we do not know when he acknowledged to himself that he was a secret disciple of
Jesus.   But the timid scholar was won to Christ.

8.   Rivalling the Baptist (3 : 22–36).

Jesus is now out of Jerusalem, but still busy in
Judea and making a tremendous sensation as He
had down in the city of His fathers.   John the Baptist had kept on with his work as was best to avoid
the appearance of pique at the success of the Messiah whose Forerunner he was.   John went on up to
Ænon near to Salim in Samaria where the abun-
dance of water served the purpose of baptizing as well

[1] 3 : 18, τοῦ μονογενοῦς υἱοῦ.   Cf. 1 : 18.

as the Jordan had done. We had seen him last at
Bethany in Perea. But the very success of Jesus
raised questionings in the minds of some of John's
followers who sought to stir up jealousy in his heart
towards Jesus and even blamed John for having borne
witness to Him (3 : 26). Nothing in John's life is
nobler than the way in which he spurned this subtle
temptation.[1] He repeated his denial of any claim to
be the Messiah himself, as whom he had joyfully
hailed Jesus. For himself he was content and glad
to be the friend of the Bridegroom, rejoicing at the
music of His words. Besides, he saw clearly that
he, like the morning star, was to fade before the Sun
who was now filling the horizon with His glory.
Verses 31–35 may be the further words of the Baptist or the meditation of the evangelist on the incident. But here again Jesus is pictured as the Son
of God, belief in whom brings eternal life.

9. The Samaritan Welcome to the Messiah (4 : 1–42).

Jesus succeeded only too well in Judea and finally
had to leave for Galilee unless He were willing to
bring things to an issue with the Pharisees at once.
John the Baptist had already been shut up in prison
in Machærus by Herod Antipas (Luke 3 : 19 f.) for
his bold denunciation of the marriage with Herodias,
both of them having divorced their spouses for the
purpose, like some modern marriages. It is probable that the Pharisees had somehow inveigled John

[1] Cf. Robertson, "John the Loyal," Chapter VII.

into the clutches of Herodias. The Pharisees are now jealous of Jesus and so He goes north through Samaria (4 : 1–4). The Samaritans did not object if travellers passed out of Judea through Samaria, only if they went towards Judea. The ministry of Jesus in Samaria is only an incident by the way as He went back to Galilee. The disciples evidently did not expect it, for they exhibit surprise that Jesus, a rabbi, should speak to a Samaritan and in public with a woman (4 : 27), contrary to Jewish customs and prejudices. The woman herself had expressed like surprise (4 : 9) and note also the evangelist's parenthetical explanation of the hostility between the Jews and the Samaritans. Jesus was a Jew in His human birth, but He was the Son of man in reality and in His sympathy and outlook. He even piqued her curiosity about the living water which He could give for the asking. So he had no hesitation about revealing Himself to this wicked Samaritan woman as the Messiah expected alike by Jew and Samaritan (4 : 25), though He expressly asserted that salvation is of the Jews (4 : 22) and so took the Jewish side in the famous controversy. But Jesus is keen to show also that God is spirit and to be worshipped by our spirits and that His worship is independent of temple or mountain. The conversion of this woman brought rare joy to the soul of Jesus and showed that His kingdom would be cosmopolitan in fact (4 : 27–38). Every soul-winner knows how to appreciate the joy of Jesus here in saving this soul from ruin. The Samaritans who are won to Jesus as the Messiah by this woman's zeal proclaim Him as " indeed the Saviour of the world" (4 : 39–42).[1]   It was easy for them to make the world-wide application of His mission so as to include themselves.   Progress is thus made in the reception of Jesus not only as the Messiah of Israel, but the Saviour of mankind, that is, of men of all races and ages.   He is no local, or national, or racial Redeemer, but the one and only Saviour for all time.

10.   The Welcome in Galilee (4 : 43–54).

The very popularity of Jesus had led Him to leave Judea because of the jealousy of the Pharisees.   A prophet, as a rule, had no honour in his own country. Hence it seemed safe for Jesus to go back to Galilee, His home land.   But an element of surprise awaits Him there, for the Galileans, who had heard Him and seen His signs in Jerusalem at the passover, had brought the great news back with them to Galilee.   Hence the fame of Jesus in Jerusalem made Him known in Galilee before He came to Cana again where His first miracle was wrought.   It is to be noted that the Gospel of John, though written primarily to prove the deity of Christ, has no hesitation in recording instances of the limitations of Jesus because of His humanity.   Indeed, one may say that the writer takes pains to show the reality of His humanity against the Docetic Gnostics who denied it.   For instance, note the weariness

[1] $\dot{a}\lambda\eta\theta\hat{\omega}\varsigma\ \dot{o}\ \sigma\omega\tau\dot{\eta}\rho\ \tauo\hat{v}\ \kappa\dot{o}\sigma\mu o\upsilon.$

of Jesus at Jacob's well (4 : 6), His hunger and thirst, and His joy at the woman's conversion. So here we have the apparent surprise of Jesus at His welcome in Galilee as later we have His emotion at the grave of Lazarus and the reality of His blood at His death. In the Gospel of John the humanity of Jesus is just as actual as His deity. Westcott notes that in the First Epistle of John the deity of Christ is assumed and His humanity is proven, just the reverse of the situation in the Gospel of John. The writer makes no effort to explain how these things can be, but modern science has revived our sense of wonder and we are not so sceptical of what we cannot understand or explain. We do not understand either the nature of man (as spirit and matter) or the nature of God (as infinite). There is small surprise that the combination puzzles our intellect sorely. But our intellects have so many limitations that we are learning modesty in the use of them. The conduct of the nobleman[1] of Capernaum is one illustration of the enthusiasm in Galilee towards Jesus at this early stage of His work there. Jesus (4 : 48) does not wish to minister to popular excitement as a mere miracle-monger, but the man's evident sincerity wins the day. Galilee is apparently ripe for receiving Jesus as Messiah. The work seems to be hastening on all sides.

[1] βασιλικός. An attendant at court, possibly at the court ot Herod Antipas.

III

THE GROWING HATRED OF JESUS
(Chapters 5–11)

*" I have believed that thou art the Christ,
the Son of God."*

THE increasing revelation of Himself as the Messiah, the Son of God, and the growing recognition of the claims of Jesus rapidly increased the hostility of the ecclesiastics in Jerusalem. In particular the Pharisees were enraged at the power of Jesus with the people, for He seemed the antithesis of all their hopes and plans. We do not know the precise length of time covered by chapters 5–11 in John's Gospel. It was certainly two years because of the three passovers in 2 : 22 ; 6 : 4 and 12 : 1. If the feast in John 5 : 1 is a passover, or if there is an unmentioned passover, then we have three years. At any rate John selects here what he considers the crucial events in the unfolding of Christ's mission in addition to those in the Synoptic Gospels, having only one miracle contained there (John 6 : 1–15). The scene of the events given by John oscillates between Jerusalem and Galilee, though mostly in Jerusalem.

1. **The Claim of Equality with God** (Chap. 5). As Jesus went up to Jerusalem on purpose to attend this feast, it was probably passover, pentecost,

or tabernacles. The healing of the impotent man by
the Pool of Bethesda might have been passed by if it
had not taken place on the Sabbath (5 : 9) and
if also the healed man had not carried his pallet
(bed) on the Sabbath as Jesus had directed him.
He seems to be a rather ingenuous sort of a fellow
and did not even know who it was that had healed
him and had bidden him violate the Pharisaic rules
concerning the Sabbath. They probably had their
suspicions as to who the man was who had thus de-
fied them right in Jerusalem by the Temple. They
evidently made the healed man feel quite uncom-
fortable, for, as soon as he saw Jesus again and
learned His name, with curious ingratitude he ran
and told the Pharisees so as to throw all the blame
on his benefactor. This fellow's infirmity was due
to personal sin, but he apparently did not heed the
warning of Jesus (5 : 14) if one may judge by his
conduct. He showed no sign of a new heart and
life. The healing of the body did not mean the
healing of the soul. He was slow-witted at any
rate. But he drops out of sight and the Pharisees (the Jews) turn their attention to Jesus, the
cause of the trouble. They were used by now to
the fact of the miracles of Jesus which they had
already begun to ascribe to the prince of the demons who worked through Jesus (Matt. 9 : 34).
So they " began to persecute ¹ Jesus because he
was in the habit of doing ² these things on the Sab-

---

¹ ἐδίωκον. Inchoative imperfect.
² ἐποίει. Customary action.

bath " (5 : 16).   The Sabbath controversy grew very keen for the Pharisees now hated Jesus very much. His defense angered them more than the offense: " My Father worketh even until now and I work." This claim of equality with the Father and the corresponding right to work on the Sabbath as God continues His creative activity did not escape the notice of His enemies.   They " sought the more [1] to kill him " (5 : 18), having already had murder in their hearts.   Religious persecutors are usually men of strong convictions of their own orthodoxy and infallibility, but with weak ethical principles.   These men felt evidently that they were the champions of God against a Sabbath-breaker and a blasphemer who happened, however, to be the Son of God Himself and who was in reality doing the very will of God.   So they pressed against Jesus " because he not only brake [2] the Sabbath, but also called God his own [3] Father, making himself equal [4] with God " (5 : 18).

Certainly Jesus is fully aware of the serious nature of the charge.   He has evidently meant for them to see what He really claims to be.   Jesus now avoids further use of the term Messiah in His claim because that has a political meaning and plays more into the hands of His enemies.   The

---

[1] μᾶλλον ἐζήτουν.   Conative imperfect.

[2] ἔλυε.   Customary action.

[3] ἴδιον because Jesus said μου.

[4] ἴσον τῷ θεῷ.   Cf. Phil. 2 : 6 ; ἴσα θεῷ.   Associative instrumental case.

claim to deity is theological and narrows the
issue between Jesus and the Pharisees. The usual
claim of Jesus to be the Son of man is in reality
Messianic though in a veiled form that the Pharisees cannot well attack. The charge of blasphemy is involved here, but the Pharisees must
prove the charge if they formally make it. The reply of our Lord to the Pharisees (5 : 19–47) is a
great apologetical exposition of His claim to
equality with God and completely silences His
enemies, though they are in no wise convinced.
The explanation comes first (19–30). Here Jesus
constantly refers to Himself as " the Son " and
speaks of God as " the Father " and thus reiterates
His previous claim of equality with God. But He
gives various details of great moment. The Son's
deeds are precisely those of the Father (5 : 19), as,
for instance, healing the impotent man on the Sabbath. The son has open access to the love,[1] knowledge, and power of the Father, and this case of the
impotent man is a small matter compared with what
the Son will do " that ye may marvel "[2] (5 : 20). As
for instance He will even raise the dead (5 : 21), as
He had already done in the case of Jairus' daughter
(Mark 5 : 35–42). The Son is the Judge of mankind (John 5 : 22). There is no honouring the Father without honouring the Son (5 : 23) and thus
the Pharisees are dishonouring God in not honour-

[1] φιλεῖ here, not ἀγαπᾷ, from φίλος friend.
[2] ἵνα ὑμεῖς θαυμάζητε. Continue to wonder. Durative
action.

ing Jesus, a pertinent word for present-day theology
which so often patronizes Jesus. Belief in the Son
brings eternal life and escape from spiritual death.[1]
Apparently (note " and now is ") in verse 25 Jesus is
claiming power over spiritual life, though in 28 f. He
undoubtedly refers to the resurrection from the tomb.
One may note also the resurrection of both classes
in 29. In verse 26 Jesus claims to " have life in
himself "[2] as the Father has. All of these are
attributes of deity and are meant by Jesus to be
so understood. It is only in the matter of judg-
ing man that Jesus explains that this power is given
Him by the Father " because he is a Son of man "
(5 : 26).[3] This is certainly a tremendous claim and
not compatible with any theory that Jesus is only a
man, even the best of men. In fact, Jesus expressly
asserts that His work has value because He sustains
this very relation to the Father and does His
will (5 : 30).

Such a claim calls for proof. This Jesus recognizes and proceeds to give (31–47). His witness
will not be accepted as true (5 : 31), He knows, if
He only bears witness of Himself. The proof that
Jesus offers is that of " another "[4] (5 : 32). He is

[1] Note two senses of death and life in this paragraph (literal
and spiritual) in 21, 24, 25, 26, 28, 29.

[2] ζωὴν ἔχειν ἐν ἑαυτῷ.

[3] υἱὸς ἀνθρώπου, not ὁ υἱὸς τοῦ ἀνθρώπου. The Aramaic *barnasha*, son of man, is ambiguous, but it is note-
worthy that the Gospel of John notes the difference so care-
fully in the Greek idiom.

[4] ἄλλος. Another of like veracity with Jesus.

glad to point to the testimony of the Baptist, to
whom the Sanhedrin had sent an embassy, and in
whose light they were all willing enough to rejoice for a season (32–35), this " burning and shin-
ing lamp."[1]   But Jesus has more than the witness
of man, even of so good and great a man as John.
He has that of the Father Himself by the very
works of Jesus which show that the Father has set
His seal of approval upon Him (36–38).   In verse
37 Jesus may by implication refer to the voice of
approval at His baptism, but at any rate He pointedly claims acquaintance with the Father and His
Word, which the Jewish leaders do not possess.
They prove their lack of connection with God by
refusal to believe God's " Apostle "[2] to them (verse
38) who was now addressing them.   But this is not
all.   Jesus has the witness of the Scriptures which
they profess to know and to " search "[3] to find
eternal life.   These very Scriptures testify of Jesus
(cf. Luke 24 : 27), but their stubbornness blinds
their eyes and paralyzes their wills.[4]   They prefer
death to life at His hands.   In particular, Moses
rises up to accuse them, Moses who wrote of Him
in his writings as the Prophet (Deut. 18 : 15) whom
they should receive (verses 41–47).

2.   **The Clamor of the Multitude** (6 : 1–15).
The scene changes to the Sea of Galilee on a

[1] ὁ λύχνος ὁ καιόμενος καὶ φαίνων.   His lamp still shines
on through the ages.   [2] ὃν ἀπέστειλεν ἐκεῖνος.
[3] ἐραυνᾶτε.   Probably present indicative.
[4] οὐ θέλετε ἐλθεῖν πρός με.

grassy slope on the northeastern side near Bethsaida-Julias in the tetrarchy of Philip. There is a
great multitude who are carried away by the words
and the deeds of Jesus. The great Galilean ministry lies behind this day (see Mark 1 : 14–6 : 13;
Matt. 4 : 12–13 : 58; Luke 4 : 14–9 : 9). The feeding of the five thousand men, besides the women
and children, was the climax. "When therefore
the people saw the sign which he did, they said,
This is of a truth the prophet that cometh into the
world" (6 : 14). This was a popular description of
the Messiah (cf. Matt. 11 : 3; John 11 : 27). In
Galilee, as we know, Jesus had been avoiding the
term Messiah and the Pharisees had tried to destroy
His power with the people by saying that He was
in league with Beelzebub (Matt. 12 : 24; Mark
3 : 22). But here the people renounce the Pharisaic
tutelage and in ecstasy of enthusiasm propose to
"seize"[1] Jesus "in order to make him king"[2]
whether or no. They are just at the point[3] of start-
ing this enterprise when Jesus perceives[4] it in time
to nip it in the bud. It is a crisis and calls for instant action on the part of Jesus. These people
have the notion of a political Messiah which the
Pharisees had taught them, which even the disciples

[1] ἁρπάζειν. Common in the papyri for violent seizure.
Cf. P. Par. 66 8 f. (Moulton & Milligan, Vocabulary of the
Greek Testament).

[2] ἵνα ποιήσωσιν βασιλέα. Note aorist tense of instant
action.

[3] μέλλουσιν.   [4] γνούς.

held in spite of Christ's teaching till the Holy Spirit came (cf. Acts 1 : 6). They planned a political coup, so to speak, and were going to take Jesus to Jerusalem and proclaim Him King in opposition to Cæsar and so throw off the hated Roman yoke. It had come to this that the Galileans would welcome Jesus as Messiah in defiance of the Pharisees if Jesus would be their sort of a Messiah. In truth, the Pharisees themselves would have hailed Him as Messiah on the same terms. It was the voice of the people, but, alas, not the voice of God. John does not tell about the sending of the multitude away (Matt. 14 : 22 f.; Mark 6 : 45), but only of the withdrawal of Jesus " again into the mountain himself alone "[1] (John 6 : 15). He was absolutely alone in the world so far as human understanding went, for the Twelve themselves evidently sympathized with the mad purpose of the crowd to make Jesus a political King in Jerusalem.

3.   The Fear of the Disciples (6 : 16–21).

Delayed by the sudden storm on the lake and the thick darkness the disciples about the fourth watch (three o'clock at night) see what looks like a ghost (Mark 6 : 49) walking on the sea and " drawing nigh[2] unto the boat." " They became[3] afraid " and naturally so. They were willing[4] to take Jesus into the boat only after His reassuring voice. John

---

[1] $\alpha\dot{v}\tau\dot{o}\varsigma$ $\mu\acute{o}\nu o\varsigma$. For He had also sent the disciples across the lake.

[2] $\gamma\iota\nu\acute{o}\mu\epsilon\nu o\nu$. Coming closer and closer.

[3] $\dot{\epsilon}\varphi o\beta\acute{\eta}\theta\eta\sigma\alpha\nu$. Ingressive aorist.   [4] $\ddot{\eta}\theta\epsilon\lambda o\nu$.

touches this miracle lightly (cf. Matt. 14 : 24–34), but it is clear that the disciples gained a fresh impression of the power of Jesus over wind and wave as they had just seen His mastery in the matter of the loaves and the fishes.

4.   The Sifting of the People (6 : 22–71).

In the synagogue in Capernaum on the morrow Jesus faces a great crowd, including the people who the day before showed such fanaticism because of the loaves and the fishes.   The populace are fickle and even now seem to be hinting for a fresh meal at the hands of Jesus.   There is not here space to follow in detail the steps by which Jesus almost casts pearls before swine in His patient endeavour to help these people see what sort of a Messiah He really is in contrast to their political hopes expressed the afternoon before.   When He seeks to turn their thoughts to the food for eternal life (26 f.), and belief on Him as sent of God (28 f.), they actually demand a new sign for such faith, something on a par with the manna in the wilderness which came every morning, not one meal on an afternoon (30 f.).   When Jesus offers them better bread than that, they eagerly cry for it, thinking only of literal bread (32–34).   But when He explains that He is Himself the bread of life and the water of life (35–40), they murmur[1] like a swarm of bees with sceptical scorn at His divine claims, this Jesus " whose father and mother we know " (41 f.).   Here

---

[1] ἐγόγγυζον.   An onomatopoetic word like our murmur.

we face the popular incredulity of the possibility of
the combination in one person of God and man.
Modern unbelief illustrates precisely the same attitude of mind.   But Jesus explains the folly of their
scorn (43) and their impotence to come to Him for
life without the drawing [1] of the Father (44).   They
are not taught of God (45).   So Jesus repeats His
claim to be the bread of life in His own flesh, which
He is giving for the life of the world (46–51).   The
Jews were indignant at this presentation of the matter and actually came to blows [2] (a sort of riot) with
each other at the idea of eating His flesh as if they
were cannibals (52).   When Jesus further explained
that they must eat His flesh and drink His blood
(53–59), it was plain that He was far beyond the
depth of these people without mystical insight.   It
is not necessary to see here a forecast of the Lord's
Supper, but simply a mystical and bold statement
of the necessity of the spiritual appropriation of the
life and death of Christ.   He even says " eateth
me." [3]   It is evident that Jesus is testing this crowd
to the bottom to see how they will rally to a spiritual Messiah.   It was only too clear what they
would do by what they did.   Many of the pro-
fessed disciples now followed the other Jews in dis-
gust out of the synagogue (66).   " They walked no
more with Jesus."   If this is all that He meant to
do, they had had enough of Him and of His message.   Now at last they had their eyes opened.

   All had gone save the Twelve.   Jesus turned to

[1] ἑλκύσῃ.   [2] ἐμάχοντο.   [3] ὁ τρώγων με.

them and asked: "Would ye also go away?"
The form[1] of the question expects a negative
answer, but the mere asking of it shows how much
Jesus took to heart this rejection by the populace
whom He longed to save.   Perhaps the Twelve had
also been disenchanted like the rest. They now
have their opportunity if they wish to leave Jesus.
It is Peter who speaks, as usual, and his answer
shows clearly that they had faced that alternative
and decided against it: " Lord, to whom shall we
go?"   That is one point.   " Thou hast the words
of eternal life."   That is another.   But best of all is
this: " And we have believed and know that thou
art the Holy One of God."   This is not a new discovery on their part.   They had seen that at the
start, but it is now their settled conviction[2] after all
their doubts and fears and they gladly reaffirm their
faith at this moment when the floating crowd have
renounced their allegiance to Jesus who is no
longer the Galilean Hero.   It is plain, therefore,
that the hope of Jesus lies in this little band of
faithful men, but there is bitterness at the bottom
of this cup of joy, for one of these men of Christ's
choice is a devil.[3]   Judas, one of the Twelve, was to
betray Jesus.   This Jesus knew, though He did not
explain the terrible accusation.   A sudden look of
dismay was probably shot at each other when Jesus
said, " one of you."

[1] μὴ καὶ ὑμεῖς θέλετε ὑπάγειν.
[2] Note perfect tenses πεπιστεύκαμεν καὶ ἐγνώκαμεν.
[3] διάβολος, not δαιμόνιον, a real υἱὸς τοῦ διαβόλου.

5. **The Ridicule of Christ's Brothers** (7: 1–10).

John skips again some six months during which time Jesus kept out of Judea as for the year before, because the Jews sought to kill Him (John 7: 1) and for most of this six months Jesus withdrew from Galilee also. The Son of man is hated in Jerusalem, disliked by many in Galilee, and now His own brothers reflect the change in the public attitude towards Jesus. They had come to feel that He was beside Himself (Mark 3: 21, 31) and now they became insolent and scornful in the sneering suggestion that Jesus was ashamed to appear in public any more and was hiding His light under a bushel. " Manifest thyself to the world," they said, " for even his brethren did not believe on him " (5: 5). This heavy additional burden Jesus had to bear, misjudgment in His own home and, for a while, even by His own mother (Mark 3: 31), the one of all others who did understand Him and believe in Him. But Jesus would walk His path alone if need be. So He did just the opposite of the impudent advice of His brothers when He did go to the feast of tabernacles. He made no claims to them.

6. **The Wrangle Over Jesus at the Feast of Tabernacles** (7: 11–8: 59).

At the feast of tabernacles six months before His death Jesus is the uppermost topic of conversation even before He comes and His enemies openly sought Him as if to kill Him (7: 11). The multitudes from Galilee and elsewhere were divided over the problem of Jesus (7 : 12), for He was now the outstanding figure of Palestine and challenged the attention of all classes. Jesus Himself was now " a sign which is spoken against " " set for the falling and the rising of many in Israel" (Luke 2 : 34), as old Simeon had said would be the case. Who is this Jesus of Nazareth whom the Jewish rulers so dislike ? This question was now to the fore in every group that gathered in the corridors of the Court of the Gentiles. But the talk was in whispers, for the friends of Jesus did not wish to play into the hands of the Jewish leaders (7 : 13). Nowhere is John more dramatic and powerful than in the swift movement of these chapters. The various elements of the national life move before us as they take various attitudes towards Jesus of Nazareth. Jesus is still the lodestone of human hearts, the standard of measurement for all modern men who cannot escape the moral appeal of the Full Stature of the Manhood of Christ (Eph. 4 : 13). Some deride, some praise and pass by, some linger and strive humbly to attain, but all notice the only Full-Grown Man of the Ages. So Jesus comes boldly to the feast in the midst of its celebration and stands in the Temple teaching without fear, though fully conscious of the electric atmosphere about Him. The hostile Jews scoff in wonder at His audacity in trying to teach without scholastic preparation or ecclesiastical permit, a sort of theological ignoramus and free-lance in their opinion (7 : 14 f.). Jesus

promptly accepts this challenge and admits the
technical correctness of their charge, but denies the
implication of ignorant invention of ill-considered
teaching because He gets His teaching directly
from God. This is a fact which they can test for
themselves by the willingness[1] to do God's will instead of mere academic disputation which gets
no whither, and thus they will find no unrighteous-
ness in Jesus (5 : 16–18). Then, while they listen
with amazement at the skill and courage of Jesus,
He suddenly charges them with failure to keep the
law of Moses which they praised so much and yet
covered up with their own pettifogging rules, a
cutting indictment of current Pharisaism in line
with that in Matthew 23 and justified by the later
Talmud itself. But like a bolt from the blue, Jesus
lets fall this question : " Why seek ye to kill me ? "
(5 : 19). The Jewish leaders are speechless at this
putting them on the defensive, this reading of their
own hearts in public. Some of the Galilean multitude, ignorant of the plans of the ecclesiastics, retort in behalf of the rulers that Jesus had a demon
(5 : 20), a favourite " fling " in those days on the part
of exasperated disputants. Certainly there is no lack
of heat in the discussion. The sparks fly fast.
Jesus refers to the one great work done by Him
probably a year and a half ago when they tried to
kill Him in Jerusalem (5 : 18) and once more justifies

---

[1] ἐάν τις θέλη—ποιεῖν. Not a mere periphrastic future,
but " the will to obey." It is in the will that the decision
of life is made. Cf. " The Will to Believe."

His habit of healing on the Sabbath day by the practice of circumcision on the Sabbath, when one Mosaic law overrides another (7 : 21–24). They are entirely too superficial in their criticism, as is the way of carping critics. The Jerusalem populace, who know of the plans of the rulers, next comment in wonder on the failure of the rulers to arrest Jesus after all their boasts and tauntingly ask if they " have come to know [1] of a truth that this fellow [2] is the Messiah " (7 : 25 f.). They add a bit of popular theology of a piece with the advice of the devil to Jesus to let the people see Him drop down from the pinnacle of the Temple as if from heaven. The people and some of the Pharisees thought that the Messiah would drop out of the skies (7 : 27). The reply of Jesus, in which He claims a knowledge of God which this mob does not possess, angers them so that they try to kill Him without waiting on the rulers (7 : 28–30). The pot is boiling now. The Galilean multitude is divided over Jesus, but many more openly champion His cause and pertinently ask whether, if Jesus is not the Messiah, the Messiah Himself will do more signs (7 : 31). This espousal of Christ leads the Pharisees to order the arrest of Jesus by Roman " officers," while Jesus calmly teaches on in defiance of their efforts. The Pharisees sneeringly explain the words of Jesus as the counsel of despair and a flight to the dispersion of the Jews among the Greeks (7 : 32–36). But

---

[1] ἀληθῶς ἔγνωσαν. Effective aorist and timeless.
[2] οὗτος in derisive mood.

Jesus is not arrested and on the last day of the feast proclaims that He has the water of life for all who will come;[1] and once again the multitude are keenly divided over Jesus as to whether He is the Christ, some explaining that the Messiah comes from Bethlehem while Jesus is from Galilee (7 : 37–44). So men argued in their ignorance, but the hands of men were stayed from Jesus for His hour was not yet come. The officers did come finally to report to the Sanhedrin, but they did not bring Jesus and bore witness to the power of Christ's words. The rage of the Pharisees reveals their scorn of Jesus and of the accursed multitude (the 'Am-ha-'Aretz, the people of the land), who alone follow the up-start Galilean (7 : 45–49). But Nicodemus, who has now won more courage, dares to make a point of law in behalf of Jesus and justice, only to bring down a fresh vial of wrath on his own head (7 : 50–52).

The feast of tabernacles is over and the crowds from abroad go home, but Jesus lingers on a few days. The Pharisees are full of resentment at the turn of affairs and very inflammable and explosive.[2] Jesus is again in the Temple when the Pharisees are. He probably said: " I am the light of the

---

[1] On each of the first seven days of this feast water from the Pool of Siloam was carried in a golden pitcher before a procession. On the eighth day this was not done, for the people were now supposed to be in the land of springs.

[2] The incident of the adulterous woman (7 : 53–8 : 11) is almost certainly not a part of the Gospel of John, though it bears every mark of being a veracious story.

world " (8 : 12) on purpose for them to hear. This
is precisely what the Pharisees thought that they
were, though they would hardly say it in plain
terms. But such a claim from Jesus, who was
taboo in Pharisaic circles, was intolerable. They
were quick to take Jesus up and to accuse Him
of simply praising Himself (8 : 13). His bare word
was not acceptable. We are bound to admit the
technical justice of this retort of the Pharisees. If
Jesus is only a man, it is well-nigh impossible to
justify such language in His mouth. The claim is
universal, for all the world and for all time. It is
only consonant with the fact of the deity of Jesus
and the revelation of this truth on the part of Jesus,
and thus follows naturally without the conceit which
would otherwise be inevitable. Jesus replies that
He can speak the truth all by Himself, but admits
their right to demand confirmation which He pro-
duces in the witness of His Father (8 : 14–18). At
this turn the Pharisees throw in His face the charge
of being a bastard [1] : " Where is thy Father ? " with
a grin and a leer (8 : 19). But Jesus witheringly
adds that they know neither Him nor His Father
(8 : 19), meaning God.

The Master seems to be in a provocative mood
and draws the lines of cleavage very sharply between Himself and the Pharisees in destiny, in
origin, in spirit (8 : 21–30). He defiantly tells them
that they shall die in their sins unless they believe
in Him. His language (8 : 24) is absolute : " That

[1] As is done in the Talmud.

I am " [1] and may be itself a claim to deity, though
Jesus stoutly refuses to say the word " Messiah " to
them or to explain further when they pointedly ask
Him: " Who art thou ? " (8 : 25). He does say
that they shall come to know who He is when they
have lifted Him up on the Cross (8 : 28), as many
did at Pentecost and afterwards (Acts 2–6).

Some of the Pharisees had been impressed by
the tremendous claims of Jesus and expressed belief in Him as the Messiah (8 : 30), but Jesus was
suspicious of the Jerusalem Pharisees (cf. 2 : 23–25)
and proceeded to test the reality and sincerity of
their faith (8 : 31–59). He wishes no disciples under
false pretenses. The only real disciples are those
who hold out and stand by the word of Jesus
(8 : 31). Thus they will know the truth and the
truth will make them free (8 : 32). Nothing else
liberates the spirit of man from the bondage of sin
and the shackles of human prejudice. At once it
is clear that these " disciples " are more Pharisee
than Christian, for they resent the implication that
they had ever been " in bondage to any man,"
though at that moment they were under the
political yoke of Rome and the still heavier religious yoke of the rabbis in spite of their pride
in being " Abraham's seed " (8 : 33). Jesus explains that they are in bondage to sin and repeats
that the Son can set them free from that, although
they (the Pharisees) were seeking to kill Him, clear
proof that their father is not the same as His Father

[1] ὅτι ἐγώ εἰμι.

(8 : 34–38). In spite of their plea that Abraham is
their father (8 : 39), they do not act like it (8 : 40)
and do the works of their spiritual father (8 : 41).
In a flash they deny that they are the children of
fornication, as by implication Jesus is (for Jesus
passed as the son of Joseph begotten out of wed-
lock). They now claim God as their " one Father "
(8 : 41). Once more Jesus explains that their conduct shows that God is not their spiritual Father,
but on the contrary proves that the devil is their
spiritual father (8 : 42–47). This was a terrific turn
of the argument against these claimants of exclusive spiritual prerogatives as the children of
Abraham. John the Baptist had called them
broods of vipers (Matt. 3 : 7), but this indictment
was far worse. Jesus had practically also accused
the Pharisees of being liars while asserting sinless-
ness for Himself. The Pharisees hiss back the
bitter words : " Say we not well that thou art a
Samaritan and hast a demon ? " (8 : 49), the two
meanest things that they can think of in their rage.
But Jesus proceeds and claims to be able to prevent death (spiritual death, of course), while the
Jews accuse Jesus of claiming to be greater than
Abraham and the prophets (8 : 50–53). This is
precisely what Jesus did claim. He must speak
the truth about Himself as God's own Son, else be
silent and so a liar like them, for Abraham rejoiced
to see His day (8 : 54–56). The Jews are literalists
and at the final claim of Jesus to timeless and
eternal existence before the day of Abraham, they

take up stones to stone Him as a common blasphemer (8 : 57–59). Jesus escaped, but the stinging memory of that day would not pass from the minds of the Pharisees.

7. The Wit of the Man Born Blind (Chap. 9).

This chapter relieves the tension of the story by the delightful play of wit and humour on the part of the gifted man who was healed by Jesus as he passed out of the storm in the Temple (9 : 1). The man's humour appears in his naive confession to his neighbours that he is in reality the very beggar who used to be blind (9 : 9). He tells the simple straightforward story of the facts relative to the opening of his eyes, sticks to it all the time, parries every effort to get himself tangled in his words, expresses his own opinion that Jesus is a prophet, refuses to call Jesus a sinner to relieve the Pharisees of their own theological embarrassments over a stubborn fact that upset their theology about the Sabbath, stands by the crucial fact of his receiving sight at the hands of Jesus, playfully twits the Pharisees with the desire to become the disciples of Jesus, makes merry over their ignorance about Jesus, and finally argues conclusively to show that God must be with Jesus at any rate. The Pharisees lose all self-control and blaze out at Him : " Thou was altogether[1] born in sin, and dost thou teach us ? " (9 : 34). They finished the business by cast-

[1] ὅλος. Every whit of you. Total depravity with a vengeance.

ing the impudent upstart out of the Synagogue
(out of church), the way of the bigot in all ages
who tries to stifle truth by injury to the herald
of it.

But the outcome of this story (9: 35–41) is beautiful indeed.   Jesus heard of the poor fellow's treat-
ment and sought him out.   He had been turned out
of the Jewish " church," but Jesus was going to take
him into the kingdom of heaven, which, alas, was
outside of that " church," as has often been true
through the ages.   Even organic Christianity has
sometimes turned the followers of Jesus out-of-doors
and left Jesus Himself standing on the outside of
the church and would not open the door to let Him
in (Rev. 3: 20), because to do that would be to dis-
turb the smug complacency of a dead church in the
grip of the devil.   So Jesus reveals Himself to the
man, whose eyes He had opened, as the Son of God
and at once receives the fealty and the worship of the
man's heart.   Here we have a flash-light on the historic environment of Jesus.   The religious leaders
of the Jewish people, who should have been able
to recognize Him as the Messiah, the Son of God,
were so utterly blind that they could not tell light
from darkness.   They even try to put out the Light
of the world and to ostracize these who have their
eyes opened to see.   They preferred the aristocracy
of darkness and death to the democracy of light,
freedom, and life in Christ.   " Are we also blind ? "
the Pharisees pitifully asked Jesus.   Alas, if their
blindness had been only intellectual and not spiritual,

their case would have been better.   They claim to be
the torch-lights of truth for the people.   They boast
of their insight and cannot escape their sin.   This
word of Jesus holds good of all preachers and theological teachers to-day.   We must all speak what
we see, but we do it at our own risk.   The Light
has come, but " men loved the darkness rather than
the light; for their works were evil" (4 : 19).

8.   A Schism by an Allegory (10: 1–21).

It is clear that the Pharisees are present.   Jesus
tells the Allegory [1] of the Good Shepherd.   He evidently tells it to draw the distinction sharply between
the Pharisees and Himself.   His sheep, like the man
born blind, hear His voice and come at His call.
The Pharisees are too dull and too prejudiced to
understand the words of Jesus (10 : 6) and so He
tells the story over again with more detail (7–18).
He explains that He is the Good Shepherd who
lays down His life for the sheep and does not run
from the wolf when he comes.   He lays down His
life voluntarily and therein lies its moral value.   He
has power also to take it up again, as He will do,
and therein lies the supreme proof of His claim to
be the Son of God able to make the atoning sacrifice for the sin of the world.   For He has other
sheep outside of the Jewish fold, Gentiles, whom He
must bring.   " I came that they may have life, and

---

[1] παροιμία (10 : 6), a word by the way, a byword, a
proverb, a parable, and here an allegory which is a self-
explanatory parable.

may have it abundantly[1]" (10:10). Out of these
separate folds will be made " one flock" under the
" one shepherd," another figure in the Kingdom of
God composed of the redeemed of all nations and
ages. Both times Jesus has indicated that the
Pharisees are like the thieves and robbers on the
outside of the Kingdom of God, and yet some of
them were convinced by the words of Jesus and in
reply to the sneer that Jesus has a demon and is
mad (both, as was usually the case) calmly assert
that Jesus has not talked like a demoniac, and, besides, " Can a demon open the eyes of the blind?"
Thus a "schism"[2] arose among the Pharisees, a
great triumph for Jesus under all the circumstances.
But all along we see that everything in this Gospel
turns round the Person of Jesus Christ.

9. An Argumentum ad Hominem (10: 22–39).

Three months apparently intervene between verses
21 and 22 in chapter 10, an interval probably spent
in Judea (Luke 10: 1–13: 21). It is now the feast
of dedication, about our Christmas time. Jesus is
walking in Solomon's porch and the Jews make a
circle[3] round Him as if they are delighted to see
Him. In fact their question means that the " sus-
pense "[4] has been unbearable and now they must
know once for all the truth about Him: " If thou

---

[1] περισσόν. An overflow of life.
[2] σχίσμα. A split.   [3] ἐκύκλωσαν.
[4] τὴν ψυχὴν ἡμῶν αἴρεις. He held their souls in mid-air
and gave them no rest.

art the Messiah tell us plainly"[1] (10: 24). It was all plausible enough and would probably have availed for the ordinary teacher, but it was a skillful trap, all the same, set right before the bird that they wished to catch. They wished Jesus to confess in plain words that He claimed to be the Messiah so that they could arraign Him before the Sanhedrin on this confession. It was not blasphemy to be the Messiah, to be sure, but this fact was inconceivable in the case of Jesus. But Jesus saw through the plot and declined to be caught in their toils. He reminded them of His previous discourses three months before and repeated some of His sayings and pointedly said: "I and the Father are one" (10: 30). This admission they at once interpreted as blasphemy and they took up[2] stones again (cf. 8: 59). But Jesus was unafraid and proceeded to "rally" them for their logical inconsistency even as they stood with stones in their uplifted hands ready[3] to hurl at Him. Granted that He did claim the term "God" for Himself by saying: "I am Son of God."[4] That language is not equal to what occurs in Psalm 82: 6 where the judges of Israel, as God's agents, are called "gods." It was a clever

---

[1] παρρησία. Fully, holding nothing back. Mr. E. S. Buchanon reports that a Western text from Armagh reads: "If thou art God, tell us plainly."

[2] ἐβάστασαν, not ἦραν of 8 : 59. It is originally to "lift" as here and later to "carry." Both uses in the papyri.

[3] λιθάζετε. Conative (present indicative) or interrupted action. The process had already begun.

[4] Note υἱὸς τοῦ θεοῦ, not ὁ υἱὸς τοῦ θεοῦ.

turn and a justifiable *argumentum ad hominem*.
As a mere man, Jesus could speak of Himself as
" a Son of God." The stones seem to have dropped
from their hands as the result of it. Certainly Jesus
did not mean to say that this was the only sense in
which He was the Son of God. This apparent disclaimer is one of Schmiedel's famous " pillars " of
doubt (I call them) about Jesus.

One is devoid of a sense of humour who does
not know how to take this incident. The writer
proceeded to show how Jesus, after this bit of theological byplay after the fashion of the rabbis of
which so many specimens occur in the Talmud,
repeated His claims to oneness with the Father
(10: 38). The result was that the Jews "sought
again to take him," though they did not apparently
hurl the stones which they had before lifted up.
Jesus escaped (10: 39) out of their hand as He
had done before (8: 59), but clearly Jerusalem was
now a dangerous place for Jesus.

10. An Echo of the Baptist's Preaching (10: 40-42).

Once more after possibly some three years He is
again at Bethany beyond Jordan, in reality a refugee
from Jewish hate, here where John the Baptist had
borne his last testimony to Jesus as the Messiah, the
Son of God (1: 28, 34). The rare quality of John's
preaching is shown by the fact that many there
recalled his message about Jesus and saw that it
was true when they beheld Jesus. John's portrait

of Jesus fit the original and they believed on Jesus
because of it. Thus John's voice has kept on echo-
ing through the ages, witnessing for Jesus as the
Messiah of God.

11. The Master of Death (11 : 1–44).

This chapter has given especial offense to many
modern critics because of the part that the raising
of Lazarus is made to play in the closing days of
Christ's life, though no mention of this great event
occurs in the Synoptic Gospels. Drummond, who
argues for the Johannine authorship of the Gospel,
balks at the historicity of this miracle. There are
raisings from the dead in the Synoptic Gospels, the
daughter of Jairus (Matt. 9 : 22–26) and the son of
the widow of Nain (Luke 7 : 11–17), but they might
by a stretch be explained by the critics as cases of
swooning, while the case of Lazarus admits of no
such naturalistic explanation. One is forced to
credit Jesus with power to bring the dead to life or
to treat the narrative as legend or simply symbolic
of spiritual life. But, I submit, if one can come
with John's argument thus far without flinching, he
need not be squeamish about this famous eleventh
chapter. If Jesus is the Logos made flesh (chapter
1), the Son of God with power over life and death
as He claimed (chapter 5), why could He not do
what God can do ? It all turns on the power of
God at last, unless the narrative bears the earmarks
of myth or legend. The absence of this incident
in the Synoptic Gospels does not render it improb-

able or incredible, since, if Lazarus were still living,
they might purposely avoid it, as they omitted
Peter's name in connection with the cutting of
Malchus's ear. We know that the rulers did try to
kill Lazarus (12 : 10). I do not see how it is possible to reject this chapter and credit the rest of the
book with much value. It may be added that most
of the critics who scoff at the raising of Lazarus explain away also the resurrection of Jesus.

Jesus and the disciples were conscious of the
peril of going back to Bethany near Jerusalem from
Bethany beyond Jordan. Recent events had made
that clear (11 : 8 f.), but Jesus was not afraid to go
and Thomas finally acquiesced with the courage of
despair, for he saw only death for them all (11 : 16).
The delay of Jesus made it four days after the death
of Lazarus before He came, but Jesus held that it
was all " for the glory of God, that the Son of God
may be glorified thereby " (11 : 4). Here Jesus calls
Himself " the Son of God," though He usually said
" the Son of man." It is significant that Martha
believes that Jesus can get power from God to restore Lazarus to life (11 : 22). When Jesus claims
to be Himself the resurrection and the life and demands of Martha her faith in this claim (11 : 25 f.),
she nobly affirms as high a creed as that of Simon
Peter (Matt. 16 : 16) and under far more trying circumstances : " Yea, Lord ! I have believed [1] that
thou art the Messiah, the Son of God, he that

---

[1] πεπίστευκα. It is her settled belief. She will not shrink
in an hour like this.

cometh into the world" (11 : 27). So Martha expresses her belief that Jesus can raise her brother from the dead now because He is the Son of God. Mary is all tears and Jesus undergoes violent agitation,[1] what with Martha's courage, His own emotion, Mary's grief, and the presence of the Jews (friends of the family, but hostile to Jesus). The presence of these Jews and the anguish of the sisters made the raising of Lazarus a test of the claims of Jesus to be the Messiah, especially after what He had said to the disciples (11 : 4) and to Martha (11 : 25). Jesus is fully conscious of the issue at stake, but was never more sure of the outcome, as is shown by His deliberate preparations and the prayer of gratitude which assumes that the Father has already heard Him (11 : 38–42). The protest of Martha as she faces the actual opening of the tomb is no real discount to her noble faith, but a woman's instinctive shrinking before the almost gruesome realities of the situation. There are few more majestic moments in the life of Jesus than this when He calls for Lazarus to come forth out of the tomb. One may be sure that failure would have been heralded to the ends of the earth. Jesus spoke in a loud voice so that those present might see that Lazarus came forth in response to His

---

[1] ἐνεβριμήσατο τῷ πνεύματι καὶ ἐτάραξεν ἑαυτόν. Both verbs here express powerful emotion in the effort for self-control. He shook himself in the effort and finally burst into tears (ἐδάκρυσεν, ingressive aorist) which was some relief. See also ἐμβιμώμενος in verse 38.

command.   Jesus stood triumphant, the Master of
death and the Giver of life.

12. The Fury of the Sanhedrin (11 : 45-57).

Small wonder is it that many of the Jews who saw
Lazarus step out " bound hand and foot with grave
clothes " should believe in Jesus on the spot (11 : 45).
Some of the timid flew to the Pharisees for help, if
they had any, else they too must believe (11 : 46).
A crisis was precipitated and a formal meeting of
the Sanhedrin was called to consider what to do[1]
under the circumstances (11 : 47).   It was plain to
see that, if matters go on thus, soon the people will
proclaim Jesus as the Messiah, there will be a revo-
lution, " and the Romans will come and take away
both our place and our nation" (11 : 48).   This
they affirm with delicious naïveté, placing their own
offices before patriotism.   But Caiaphas, the high
priest, is bolder still and has a plan already.   " It is
expedient for you that one man should die for[2] the
people, and that the whole nation perish not "
(11 : 50).   It is so easy to settle a crisis by making
a sacrifice of some one else.   His words were hailed
as the acme of wisdom and from that day Jesus was
doomed by formal vote of the Sanhedrin (11 : 53).
He is now a hunted man and it is only a matter of
weeks till the inevitable end.   Once more Jesus is

---

[1] τi $\pi o \iota o \hat{\upsilon} \mu \epsilon \nu$; present indicative.   A confession that they
are doing nothing.

[2] $\hat{\upsilon} \pi \grave{\epsilon} \rho$ $\tau o \hat{\upsilon}$ $\lambda a o \hat{\upsilon}$.   An undoubted use of $\hat{\upsilon} \pi \acute{\epsilon} \rho$ in the substitutionary sense as the context makes plain.

in the hills of Ephraim near where the devil tempted
Him after His baptism (11 : 54). The passover of
destiny drew on as Jesus moved up to Galilee and
down through Perea to meet His Hour, the Hour
for which He had come to earth. The people who
had gone up to Jerusalem ahead of Him to purify
themselves for the feast sought for Him and stood
in groups in the Temple and talked of the great
crisis on hand. Would Jesus face His enemies at
the passover ? On the whole they thought He
would not.[1] The chief priests (Sadducees) and the
Pharisees (the Sanhedrin leaders) had placed a price
on His head and had advertised for His capture
(11 : 57). Probably a tablet was already placed in
the Temple courts to that effect like one discovered
in the ruins.[2]

[1] The question in 11 : 56 has μὴ and expects the answer
" No."
[2] Deissmann, " Light from the Ancient East," p. 75.

IV

THE SECRET OF JESUS
(Chapters 12–17)

" He that hath seen me hath seen the Father."

THIS section of the Gospel is often called the " Heart of Jesus." Indeed Sears termed the Fourth Gospel " The Heart of Christ." These chapters are the most familiar parts of the book and present the sympathetic side of Christ's nature quite in contrast to the militant note in chapters 5–10, but quite in the strain of chapter 11. Painters of Christ have taken their cue almost entirely from John 12–17 to the neglect of the masterful element of struggle so prominent in the earlier chapters of John and in the Synoptic Gospels. Both aspects of His character are true.[1] Jesus is both the suffering Messiah and Christus Victor. The circumstances that surround Jesus are the most affecting imaginable. He has run His race nearly to the goal. He knows what the outcome will be. He shrinks from the awful catastrophe and yet is sure of triumph. Meanwhile, He must make one

---

[1] See Selbie, " Aspects of Christ " (1909) ; Farrar, " The Life of Christ as Represented in Art ; " Matheson, " Studies in the Portrait of the Messiah " (1900); " St. John's Portrait of Christ " (1910).

12849

more effort to prepare the disciples for the gloom of
His death, all the more that one of them is to betray Him. So here we have Christus Consolator.
He is trying to give " the faith that looks through
death " for the heartening of the eleven faithful men
who go with Him down to the Valley of the Shadow
of Death.[1]

1. The Feast in Christ's Honour at Bethany (12 : 1–8).

The Gospels of Mark and Matthew record this
feast at Bethany on Tuesday evening (Roman time)
just two days before the passover (Matt. 26 : 2,
6–13; Mark 14 : 1, 6–9), while John apparently
(12 : 1) locates it six days before the passover. It is
possible, of course, that John may simply mention
the feast in connection with the statement of Christ's
arrival at Bethany since he does not again recur to
Bethany in his narrative and so out of chronological
order.   John does not state that it was at the house
of Simon the leper, but simply has " they," but notes
that Martha, Mary and Lazarus were there. For
the purpose of our discussion the point of importance is His justification of Mary's beautiful act of
high sentiment against the selfish criticism of Judas
who rallied all the apostles to his view. " Suffer her
to keep it against[2] the day of my burying " (12 : 7).

[1] See Bowen, "Love Revealed. Meditations on John
XIII–XVII " (1884); Burrell, " In the Upper Room "
(1913) ; Sample, " Christ's Valedictory ; " Swete, " The
Last Discourse and Prayer " (new edition, 1915).
[2] εἰς.

Matthew (26 : 12) and Mark (14 : 8) explain more
clearly that Jesus meant that the act of Mary was a
preparation for His burial. She alone had come to
understand the repeated predictions of Jesus about
His death reported in the Synoptic Gospels, especially during the last six months. She probably
did not understand what He meant by resurrection,
but with a woman's delicate insight Mary of Bethany had caught to some extent the point of view
of Jesus, and she showed her love and sympathy before the burial. The shadow of the Cross was thus
at this feast of gratitude, but the devil himself entered afresh into the heart of Judas (Luke 22 : 3)
and sent him in a resentful rage to the Sanhedrin
who were in despair how to accomplish the death
of Jesus. So while Mary's heart was full of tender
sympathy with Christ about His death, Judas with
murderous treachery was plotting to hasten that
death.

2. The Curiosity of the Crowd (12 : 9–11).

We must probably go back in imagination to the
Friday afternoon and the Sabbath (cf. John 12 : 12
Sunday) before the passover when Jesus is at Bethany, having come on up from Jericho (Luke 19 : 28 ;
John 12 : 1). " The common people " [1] from the
city and from a distance learned that Jesus was there
and they went out to see Jesus and to see Lazarus

---

[1] ὁ ὄχλος πολὺς (see also 12 : 12). On this idiom see
Robertson, " Grammar of the Greek New Testament," etc.,
p. 774.

who had been raised from the dead. One can easily imagine the excitement that this combination created. The raising of Lazarus had led the Sanhedrin by formal vote to decide to put Jesus to death before His arrest or trial (John 11 : 53). Now they have decided to put Lazarus to death also and for the same reason that because of him " many of the Jews went and believed on Jesus " (John 12 : 10 f.). Now all other public questions sank out of sight. The one goal before the Sanhedrin was to put Jesus out of the way and all others, if necessary, who clung to Him.

3. The Messianic Demonstration (12 : 12–19).

It is Sunday morning, not the Jewish Sabbath, when Jesus by formal act announces His claim to be the Messiah of the Jews. He allows the multitudes (chiefly from Galilee and Perea) which follow Him from the hills around Bethany and which meet Him as they come out of Jerusalem (John 12 : 13) to proclaim Him. A year before this the crowd near Bethsaida-Julias had wished to do this very thing and to make Jesus the King Messiah, but He would not then allow them to do it (John 6 : 15). But now it is clear to all who believe in Jesus that the crisis has come and that the policy of secrecy is over. The crowd at Jericho had felt that on this visit of Jesus to Jerusalem " the Kingdom of God was immediately to appear" (Luke 19 : 11). Indeed, Jesus had made deliberate preparation for this Messianic demonstration (Matt. 21 : 2 ; Mark 11 : 1f.;

Luke 19:29 f.). Jesus had in mind the prophecy
of Zechariah 9:9: "Behold the King is coming to
thee, just and saving; he is meek and riding on a
beast of burden and a young foal." Neither the disciples nor the populace seem to have understood
the significance of this detail (John 12:16). It
was only later, as so often, that they came to see
what was the appropriateness of this humble steed
in the Triumphal Entry. The people themselves
were stirred to act by the enthusiasm over the raising of Lazarus as John (12:17 f.) alone explains and
thus enables us to understand the Synoptic account
of the sudden outburst (Dods, " Expositor's Greek
Testament," in loco). The picture of Jesus on the
young ass was probably not very majestic and little
calculated to set a crowd so ablaze. And yet they
cried: " Hosanna: Blessed is he that cometh in the
name of the Lord, even the King of Israel" (John
12:13). They seized the fronds on the palm trees
which grew on the road from Jericho to Jerusalem
and carried them because palm branches were a recognized symbol of victory and joy.[1] It was all simple enough in comparison with a triumph of a Roman
general in Rome with his chariots, his trophies, and
his captives in a procession of great grandeur.
But Christ will lead Paul in His triumphal train[2]
and the mightiest of earth in course of time. There
were probably some who mocked as they swept on
round Olivet and down the Valley of Jehoshaphat

[1] Cf. Pausanias, Vol. VIII, p. 48 ; 1 Macc. 13 : 5.
[2] 2 Cor. 2 : 14.

towards the City of the Great King. Some of the
Pharisees did try to make Jesus ashamed of this spectacular performance of the rabble (Luke 19: 39 f.).
But Jesus is determined to make public defiance of
the Sanhedrin who had been so anxious to learn
who He claimed to be (John 10: 24). Now they
know. The enthusiasm of the crowd burst all
bounds (Luke 19 : 37 f.). The Pharisees indeed well
understood the meaning of this public outpouring
of the people who openly hailed Jesus as the Messiah. It meant that He was the Hero of the masses
here at the passover and that the Sanhedrin were
helpless to carry out their plans of murderous re-
venge while this multitude of sympathizers were on
hand. At the best they must postpone their plans
to kill Jesus till after the passover (Luke 19 : 47 f. ;
22 : 6). At the worst it meant the complete failure
of all their plans and the triumph of Jesus over them.
Some of the Pharisees now felt this to be the case
and in a burst of despair blamed the other Pharisees
for the victory of Christ: " Behold how ye prevail
nothing; lo, the world is gone after him " (John
12 : 19). It did look so, for the hills were covered
with the crowds that cheered Christ as He moved
on into Jerusalem and into the very courts of the
Temple where the boys[1] echoed the cry of the
throng right in the ears of the Sadducees (chief
priests) and Pharisees (scribes) who were " moved
with indignation " (Matt. 21 : 10 f., 14–17). We
need not suppose that this motley crowd of enthu-

[1] τοὺς παῖδας (Matt. 21 : 15).

siasts understood the spiritual character of the Kingdom of God whose advent they were hailing or
dreamed that Jesus was not going to be the political Messiah that they thought He was now an-
nouncing Himself to be. Even the Apostles themselves had not yet come to see the real truth about
Christ and the Kingdom. Time and the march of
events could alone prepare their hearts for the en-
lightening work of the Holy Spirit (cf. Acts 2–3).
Even to-day scholars find it difficult to interpret
rightly the teaching of Jesus concerning the Kingdom of God and His Messiahship. Some, like
Schweitzer,[1] would make the outlook of Jesus to be
purely eschatological and cataclysmic with the result that Jesus expected to the last what did not
come and died a broken and disappointed man.
But the Gospel of John certainly powerfully presents the idea of the present possession of eternal
life in Christ as the heart of the idea of the Kingdom
of God. The Kingdom is " within "[2] men's hearts,
we learn even in the Synoptic Gospels (Luke 17 : 21).
It is at bottom the rule of God in the heart of the
individual, a present reality which is eternal in its
growth and power. There are external features
connected with its expansion in society and eschatological features in its consummation. It is, however,

---

[1] " The Quest for the Historical Jesus." So also Lake,
" The Stewardship of Faith " (1915). But Sanday, " Chris-
tologies : Ancient and Modern," argues against this purely
ad interim ethics.

[2] ἐντός never means " among."

a wholly one-sided view to limit the horizon of Jesus on this subject to that of His Pharisaic contemporaries. The Jewish apocalyptic literature of the time does throw undoubted light on the terminology of Jesus and of the New Testament writers; but we are not at liberty to make Jesus, the Son of God, a merely mistaken apocalyptic dreamer who was led away by too long perusal of this type of literature and by brooding over the wrongs of His nation till the popular enthusiasm swept Him off His feet. We must look at all the aspects of this subject.[1] The Gospel of John is a lucid and powerful exposition of the spiritual aspect and present reality of the Kingdom of God. We must distinguish therefore between popular theology on the subject and the ideals of Jesus as He proclaimed Himself the Messiah of Israel.

4. The Agitation of Jesus at the Coming of the Greeks (12 : 20–36).

It was not an unknown thing for devout Greeks

[1] See Bruce, " The Kingdom of God " (1893); Dewick, " Primitive Christian Eschatology " (1912); Goodspud, " Israel's Messianic Hope to the Time of Jesus " (1900); Haupt, " Die eschatologischen Aussagen in den synoptischen Evangelien " (1895); Jackson, " The Eschatology of Jesus " (1913); Muirhead, " The Eschatology of Jesus " (1904); Oesterley, " The Apocalypse of Jesus " (1912); Sanday, " The Life of Christ in Recent Research " (1907); Scott, " The Kingdom and the Messiah " (1911); Sharman, " The Teaching of Jesus Concerning the Future " (1909); Walker, " The Cross and the Kingdom " (1902); Winstanley, " Jesus and the Future " (1913); Worsley, " The Apocalypse of Jesus " (1912).

to attend worship in Jerusalem. In the Acts we find these devout Greeks and Romans in most of the cities. They have not broken with their race connections and yet they attend worship in the synagogues and are open for the reception of the gospel. These men may have been proselytes from Decapolis or Galilee (Dods, "Expositor's Greek Testament," *in loco*). Their courteous request[1] to Philip means more than the mere desire to " see "[2] Jesus as a spectacle which they could easily do as He publicly taught in the Temple. They wish to make a call on Jesus, to " visit "[3] Him in a formal interview. Jesus had certainly been heard by Greeks in Decapolis, in Iturea, Galilee, and Phœnicia. But this formal request from Greeks to interview Jesus in Jerusalem puzzled Philip greatly, for it raised the whole problem of race prejudice and the relation of the Kingdom of God to the Gentiles. Philip sought counsel with Andrew, who had shown himself to be a man of wisdom. But even Andrew was not able to solve this knotty question. If we are surprised at the sensitive narrowness of these two apostles, we need only to recall the hatred between Jews and Samaritans, the reluctance of Peter on the housetop at Joppa (Acts 10) and his timidity before the

---

[1] The form of the Greek is a bit more abrupt than the English translation. θέλομεν is present indicative and means " we desire," but not here our blunt " we want."

[2] ἰδεῖν.

[3] From *video*, to see. For " see " in another sense cf. John 3 : 3, " See the Kingdom."

Judaizers at Cæsarea (Gal. 2 : 11 ff.), and the intensity of race feeling to-day among Christians themselves as seen in various sections and cities of the United States. The whole city of Jerusalem was ringing with talk about Jesus after the Triumphal Entry. There is no reason for surprise at the request of the Greeks. Our surprise is at the hesitation of Philip and Andrew. But they brought the problem to Jesus, as was proper, though we do not know whether they brought the Greeks along also. If Philip and Andrew came in perplexity, it was probably greatly increased by the violent agitation which Jesus displayed as the result of their inquiry. A small match or a spark can set off a powder-mill. Volcanoes of emotion are smothering in all of us. Jesus had faced the hate of races for each other. He loved the whole world and had come to save men of the whole world (John 3 : 16; 4 : 35–41; 10 : 16). But He knew also, as His disciples did not know, that nothing but His death on the Cross would ever bring men of varied races together into one flock under one Shepherd. The missionary enterprise is a corollary of the Cross. Without that there is no message and no hope. Instead of giving a direct answer to Philip and Andrew Jesus proceeded to expound the philosophy of self-sacrifice by the parable of the grain of wheat and the ear that follows its death. All at once in heart Jesus faces the Cross in an agony of suffering that causes a momentary shrinking like that in the Garden of Gethsemane as recorded in the Synoptic Gospels.

He sees His hour for glorification by death (12 : 23) and His soul is troubled and cries out for rescue, but with instant acquiescence in the Father's will (12 : 27 f.). Here the human side of Jesus comes out strongly. He is no Docetic Man. At the crisis of His earthly career Jesus realizes full well the real situation: " For this cause came I unto this hour." He had come to earth at all in order that He might meet this hour and conquer death for the redemption of men. But He trembles for the moment on the brink of the dread leap into the dark abyss. He finds comfort in the word " glorify." [1] " Father, glorify thy name." The Father answered audibly as He did at the baptism and at the transfiguration, two great crises in the Saviour's ministry : " I have both glorified it, and will glorify it again." It is the " glory " of death that is here promised Jesus, and He so understands it. That was the topic of conversation with Jesus and Moses and Elijah on the mount of transfiguration when the glory of God covered the scene. The people do not understand this message, though they hear a sound (John 12 : 29), but Jesus is heartened to go on with His task and His talk : " Now is the judgment of this world : now shall the prince of this world be cast out. And I, if I be lifted up [2] from the earth, will draw [3] all men unto myself " (12 : 31 f.). In the death of Jesus, Satan, who is the prince of this world and

---

[1] δοξάζειν. Cf. δόξα for the Shekinah.
[2] ὑψωθῶ can only refer to the Cross. Cf. 8 : 28.
[3] ἐλκύσω.

who sets the standard by which men hate each
other and kill each other, has his power broken.
This Jesus sees. By the Cross Jesus will, like the
magnet of the world, draw all kinds of men, Jew
and Greek, bond and free, male and female, to love
Him and to love each other. This Paul claimed
(Eph. 2) did come to pass by the Cross of Christ
which broke down the middle wall of partition between Jew and Gentile. It is true in spite of the
riot of hate now running over the earth in the world
war. This will pass and peace will come. Jesus
shall yet reign in the hearts of men. Then, as now,
many did not desire this sort of a Son of man who
died on the Cross (12 : 34). The suffering Messiah
formed no part of the popular theology as the new
theology to-day has no room for the atonement and
is ashamed of the Cross of Jesus as were the Jews
and Greeks in Paul's day (1 Cor. 1 : 23). But Jesus
warned the people not to sin against the light.

5. Cowardly Disciples (12 : 37–43).

The warning was needed. Some even of the
rulers who had come to believe on Jesus were yet
afraid to take their stand on His side " because of
the Pharisees," " lest they be put out of the synagogue." They cared more for social standing with
their " set" than for loyalty to Jesus. They cared
more for " the glory " [1] from men than for glory
from God. Their eyes were blinded by the God of
this world so that they were unwilling to step out

---

[1] τὴν δόξαν.

into the open on the side of Christ while He was
unpopular with the Pharisees. Jesus, as the Son
of God, the Saviour from sin to His death on the
Cross, is still *taboo* in many modern religious circles
who practise intellectual and religious ostracism as
effectually as did the Pharisees of old. In some
modern scholastic circles it is unscholarly and unscientific to advocate the deity of Jesus or the value
of the Cross. They laugh at the idea that Isaiah
saw the glory of Jesus (John 12 : 41) or that there
is much glory for any one to see to-day save that
of a well-meaning, but wholly misguided Galilean
peasant who came to imagine that He could " save "
mankind and whose martyrdom led His followers to
" deify " Him and so to start a new superstition
which the world is rapidly outgrowing by modern
knowledge which is the only light of man. And
John (or the author of this Gospel), they say, is
simply the worst of the " deifiers " of Jesus.

6. **An Epitome of Christ's Position** (12 : 44–50).
John represents Jesus as giving this summary in
one address, though some critics argue that it is a
gathering up of teachings on various occasions,
though why it is impossible for Him to have said it
at this time is not clear. Each sentence presents
sharply the claims of Jesus about Himself which
Jesus now boldly states. Faith in Jesus is faith
in God who sent Him. Seeing Jesus is seeing God.
His mission is to bring light to set men free from
darkness. Obedience to Christ is the way to escape

judgment.   Rejection of Christ is rejection of God.
He has the Father's commandment which brings
life eternal.   All of these things Jesus had spoken
at other times and they occur here and there in the
Gospel of John before this period.   Now Jesus
summed the case up between Him and the world
which was rejecting Him.   There is no escape from
the issue of Jesus.   He confronts every man in all
the world through all the ages.   He challenges
every man to-day.   What think you of Jesus the
Christ?   What will you do with Jesus the Saviour?
What shall Jesus the Judge do with you?   Dr.
Philip S. Moxom (*North American Review*, September, 1916, "A Modern Conception of God,"
p. 405) says: "But the Jesus of the Fourth Gospel is a sublime egotist, sublime but an egotist,
wholly unlike the Jesus of the Synoptists."   This is
a common superficial view of some critics.   One
need only refer to Matthew 11 : 25–30; Luke 10:
21–24;   Matthew 28 : 18–20;   Luke 24: 44–49.
And then there is the voice of the Father at the
baptism, the voice of the Father on the mount of
transfiguration, the assumption of divine power to
forgive sins (Luke 5 : 21 ff.), besides many similar
passages.   The assumption that the Synoptic Gospels present only the humanity of Jesus while the
deity of Jesus appears only in John's Gospel is utterly false.   Both features appear in Mark and in Q
(the Logia of criticism).   The shading of the picture
is different, but the Person is the same in all the
Gospels.

7. An Example of Humility (13 : 1–20).

The Gospel of John passes by the last day in the
public ministry of Jesus in the Temple, that Tuesday
of the great debate and the great eschatological discourse on the Mount of Olives, all so fully presented
in the Synoptic Gospels. It is Thursday evening
(Roman time, beginning of Jewish Friday) that John
takes up the story. Jesus is in the upper room
prepared for Him by His directions to Peter and
John (Luke 22 : 8) and possibly the home of Mary,
the mother of John Mark (Acts 12 : 12). This is
probably the regular passover meal at the customary
time and not an anticipatory meal twenty-four hours
ahead.[1] Jesus had looked forward with eagerness
(Luke 22 : 15 f.) to this last passover meal with the
men who had been with Him in His trials [2] (Luke
22 : 28). He was Himself the true Paschal Lamb to
be offered up before twenty-four hours have passed.
But a rude shock had come to Christ when He
found the Twelve contending for primacy at the
table, each one considering himself entitled to the
post of honour (Luke 22 : 24). They were, like all
Orientals and some Westerners, sensitive on this
point of etiquette and had wrangled twice before
over the question of rank among themselves as they
discussed their plans for a temporal kingdom which
was never to be (Mark 9 : 34 ; Luke 18 : 35 ff.).

[1] The Gospel of John is in real agreement with the Synoptic Gospels on this point when properly interpreted. See my
note in Broadus' "Harmony of the Gospels," pp. 253–257.
[2] πειρασμοῖς. Same word is used for temptations.

How they finally reclined we do not know except
that John was next to Jesus and leaned back on His
bosom. Da Vinci in his great picture has James on
the other side, an allusion to the ambitious request
of James and John. The strife evidently continued
during the meal and those who were disappointed
were resentful in look and word. The devil was
already in the heart of Judas who knew what he
was going to do this very night (John 13 : 2) and
he was trying to get an entrance into the hearts of
the rest through jealousy by the eye-gate and ear-
gate. Jesus is conscious [1] that His hour is near and
arises [2] during supper [3] and begins to wash the disciples' feet, evidently because the dissatisfaction
keeps up. It is hard to stop such an unpleasant-
ness. Each one wishes the last word and the last
look. The behaviour of Peter is characteristic.
But Jesus does not leave His object-lesson to teach
its own lesson. He explains it to this kindergarten
class. " Ye call me, Teacher, and, Lord : [4] and ye
say well ; for so I am." Jesus asserts and repeats
(13 : 13 f.) His claim to be " the Teacher and the
Lord." He is here like Socrates with his disciples, but far more. He is the Master in teaching
and the Lord of life. He has given them an " example " [5] of humility and commands their imitation

---

[1] Note εἰδὼς twice (13 : 1, 3).   [2] ἐγείρεται (13 : 4).

[3] δείπνου γινομένου (13 : 2).

[4] ὁ διδάσκαλος καὶ ὁ κύριος as titles, and not in apposi-
tion with με.

[5] ὑπόδειγμα like the copy-book for writing beneath the copy.

of their Master. They greatly needed this lesson
then and there, given right in the midst of the
solemn celebration of this last passover meal. An
apostle [1] such as they were is not greater than the
one who sent him. Jesus has here punctured official and ecclesiastical pride for all time. But men
have missed the point of Jesus in this very "example" and some have imagined that Jesus meant
them literally to wash each other's feet as a church
ordinance. Cessation of strife and wrangling and
coöperative service in love is the way to "copy"
Christ's example of humility. The heart of Jesus is
greatly moved, for here is Judas who has already
bargained to sell his Master to the Sanhedrin for
thirty pieces of silver, the price of a slave. "He
that eateth my bread lifteth up his heel against me"
(Ps. 40: 9). Jesus quoted these words and Judas
must have winced inwardly. In all countries it is
considered a gross breach of hospitality to eat one's
bread and then to act the part of an enemy. The
Arabs to-day count it a covenant of friendship if
one takes salt in another man's tent. It was so with
the Jews.[2] Jesus makes it plain beforehand so that
the treachery of Judas may be all the plainer.

8. The Anxiety of Jesus (13: 21–38).

Jesus is "troubled in spirit"[3] as He was by the
grave of Lazarus (11 : 33). He has said: "I know

---

[1] ἀπόστολος (13 : 16).
[2] Cf. Trumbull, "Blood Covenant," p. 313; "Oriental
Life," p. 361.   [3] ἐταράχθη τῷ πνεύματι.

whom I have chosen" (13 : 18). He assumes His
share of the responsibility for the selection of Judas,
but that fact in no wise relieves Judas of his guilt.
We are not mere automata, however much of mystery surrounds us in this world of law. A sort of
stupefaction seems to rest on the Apostles, for they
are completely taken aback by the specific statement
that the betrayer was one of their number (13 : 22).
They even fail to grasp the point of the sign of the
sop which Jesus gives to Judas or to understand
the word by which Jesus reveals to Judas knowledge
of his treachery (13 : 23–29). They are all so intent
in their suspicions [1] about each other and protesta-
tions of innocence that they fail to see what is
plainly before their eyes. But now Judas is gone
out into the night on his hellish mission (13 : 30)
and Jesus turns to the rest with something of the
feeling of a hen who has lost one of her brood to
the hawk who has scooped it away. He had so
felt about Jerusalem (Matt. 23 : 37) and now Satan
has made complete conquest of Judas (John 13 : 27).
The fact that Jesus knew all along that Judas was a
devil (6 : 70) does not lighten His sorrow, though it
does relieve Jesus of any moral responsibility
(17 : 12) for this " son of perdition." Indeed, Jesus
turns to the glorification of the Cross with a sense
of relief as Judas goes away from their number.[2]

These discourses in John 13 : 31 to 17 : 26 bear
the same relation to the Fourth Gospel that the

---

[1] ἔβλεπον. Kept looking in their perplexity (ἀπορούμενοι).
[2] Dods, " Expositor's Greek Testament," *in loco.*

eschatological discourse does to the Synoptic Gospels (Matt. 24, 25 ; Mark 13 ; Luke 21) and the two lines of thought are complementary (Westcott, *in loco*). The one deals with the outward aspects of the kingdom in the future, the other with the inward growth of the soul. The "glorification"[1] of the Son of man and of God by the death of Jesus now fills His heart. This view of His death transcends all the petty meannesses of His enemies. Jesus even says (13 : 32) that God will take up the glorified humanity of the Son of man into His own being (Westcott, *in loco*). Henceforth the humanity of Jesus will be an added glory to the Son of God (cf. Phil. 2 : 9–11). But, after this exalted word about His own relation with the Father in His death, Jesus turns again to the Eleven who are left with a promise that they shall follow Him after a while and with the command meanwhile to love[2] one another as He has loved them and so carry out "the new commandment,"[3] an eleventh commandment or summary of the Law. This very night they have already shown jealousy towards each other. The key to the work of the kingdom, after Jesus is gone, lies just here in the love of Christians for each other. But Peter passes by this command and is curious to know whither He is going and

---

[1] The aorist tense ἐδοξάσθη (13 : 31) treats the death of Christ as an accomplished fact, the glory of which Jesus already enjoys by anticipation.

[2] The word ἀγαπᾶτε is here used, the noblest love.

[3] Cf. 1 John 2 : 7–11.

why he cannot follow now since he is willing to lay
down his life for Jesus (13 : 36 f.).   So lightly does
the chief Apostle take the death of Christ and His
own courage in the face of it.   It is a painful thing
to perform a surgical operation on a man's pride,
but Jesus does it (13 : 38).   However, Peter does
not stand alone in his boasting, for all the rest join
in the promise of fidelity till death (Matt. 26 : 35),
though Peter shows more vehemence (Mark 14 : 31).
Luke reports Jesus as revealing that Satan has been
allowed[1] to "sift you[2] as wheat" and that Jesus
has made special supplication for Peter[3] (Luke
22 : 31 f.).   The anxiety of Jesus is not mere nervous apprehension.   No one knows the power of
the devil over men as does He for the very reason
that He has vanquished him.   The prescience of
Jesus was meant to put the Apostles on guard.
His prayer for Peter will bring him back after his
fall (Luke 22 : 32).   Presumption is merely weakness.

9. A Plea for Loyalty After Christ's Death (14 : 1–15 : 11).

Jesus understands the disciples better than they
do themselves.   They have made the most solemn
avowals of fealty which Jesus distrusts, but He is
not in despair about them.   The shock of His surrender when arrested, and His trial and death will be

---

[1] ἐξητήσατο.   "Got permission by asking."   Satan was
allowed to test them all and they all "left him and fled"
(Mark 14 : 50).

[2] Satan was able "to sift" (τοῦ σινιάσαι) them all.

[3] περὶ σοῦ.

greater than they can bear. They need supreme
courage and help. So Jesus talks with these eleven
men in the Upper Room which became to them a
sort of Holy of Holies in their memories of it. He
lays bare to them the secrets of His heart. He
knows that they will not understand it all, but it
will stick in their minds and come back to them by
the help of the Holy Spirit. Words of consolation
do not prevent trouble, but sympathy in the presence of death is necessary to one's breath. In a
way this is Christ's farewell talk to this group of
men about whom His hopes for the future of the
kingdom centre. He has done His best with them
and He is not sorry that He chose them rather than
others. They have their limitations and weak-
nesses, but they possess varied virtues and now the
supreme test of their lives has come. It is an un-
avoidable test for them, one that Jesus has long
foreseen and for which He has tried to prepare their
minds and hearts. A mother loves to spare her
children trouble, if she can, but the time comes
when they too must meet the issues of life and
death. So Jesus, in full view of His death, pleads
for the same faith [1] in Himself that they have in God
(14 : 1). This is, to be sure, putting Himself on a
par with God as the object of faith, but they should
be used to that idea by now. This is the real cure
for the disturbance [2] of heart which they now feel.

---

[1] This is true whether $\pi\iota\sigma\tau\varepsilon\acute{u}\varepsilon\tau\varepsilon$ be taken as indicative or
imperative or one one way and the other another way.

[2] $\tau\alpha\rho\alpha\sigma\sigma\acute{\varepsilon}\sigma\theta\omega$. Cf. our palpitation of the heart.

Jesus promises a place for each of them in His
Father's house (14 : 2). That is Christ's picture of
heaven, at home with God. He promises also to
come back and to take them to that home to be
with Him in the Father's house (14 : 3). This is
the real answer to Peter's query in 13 : 36. It is
not clear whether Jesus here means death or His
own second coming. Both are true comings of
Christ for His own. Thomas takes up the statement of Jesus about knowing the way, for he, like
Peter, is puzzled about the way to the Father's
house (14 : 4-6). Modern science has made heaven
seem very intangible and far away for many people
who sympathize with the scepticism of Thomas
about the place and the way. The answer of Jesus
to Thomas is the answer to sceptics to-day. It lies
in the realm of personality. The Father is spirit
and that means personality. Jesus Himself is the
way to the Father, the way here on earth and the
bridge to heaven at last. These words to Thomas
make Christianity intelligible to the common man
in a world of wonder and mystery. Let the phi-
losophers speculate about monism. Let the scientists find out all they can about matter. Let the
theologians theorize about the purposes and nature
of God. Jesus brings God into the vision of man
so that he can see and follow and live. " I am the
way, and the truth, and the life." [1] Jesus is each
one of these wonderful things. He is all of them

[1] Ἐγώ εἰμι ἡ ὁδὸς καὶ ἡ ἀλήθεια καὶ ἡ ζωή. Note separate article each time.

together. He is the Incarnation of God, the Personification of truth, the Energy of life. The proof of this marvellous claim can be put to the test in each man's life. Take a drunken convict like S. H. Hadley, a drunken dealer in counterfeit money like Harry Monroe, a drunken hobo like Mel. E. Trotter. They tried the way in Christ, who gave them life, and enriched their souls with truth. They have blessed thousands of other lives. It works, what Jesus says. No modern sceptic is entitled to deny it till he tries it. So George J. Romanes, the famous scientist, found his way back from doubt to God in Christ. Jesus says that there is no other way to God save through Him. This is obviously true if Jesus is the Son of God. Men who refuse to walk this way to God wander into the wilderness. It is good to think that some Unitarians like William Ellery Channing really worship Jesus in spite of metaphysical distinctions about His nature. So did the authors of " Nearer, My God, to Thee," and " In the Cross of Christ I Glory," both of whom were Unitarians. But I press to-day the point of Jesus here in John's Gospel that Jesus is the way to God for sinful men to tread and the only way.

The disciples are all alert now and realize that Jesus is dealing with the greatest problems of life. So Philip takes up the word of Jesus about knowing the Father by knowing Him[1] (13:7) and shows his

---

[1] Please note that these candid expressions of doubt come from the circle of the Twelve. Jesus treats fairly their intellectual difficulties and tries to help them into clearer light.

own failure to see the Father in Jesus though living with Him these years: " Lord, show us the Father, and it sufficeth us "[1] (13:8). Moses had once begged to see God (Ex. 33:17 ff.) and Isaiah (40:5) had promised the revelation of "the glory of Jehovah." It was a universal craving to see God, to "feel after him and find him" (Acts 17:27). Let us not be too hard on Philip who voiced their longing for an objective manifestation of God, however childish it is in reality. But the tragedy of it all is that Philip has not really known Jesus, else he would not ask such a question (14:9). It is easy to understand how natural it is for men to make idols by which to objectify God, when Philip wishes to see more of God than Jesus has brought him, had not in reality seen God in Christ.

The union of the Father and the Son is a matter of nature, but also of works, and Philip can see the works and believe that far (14:10 f.). So to-day men criticize Jesus for not being enough like God and then the Gospel of John for making Him too much like God. Jesus has made it possible to interpret God in terms of personality and not of mere abstraction. God is like Jesus. Jesus is also like God. Jesus is God.

With this conception of His Person clear Jesus goes on to plead for fidelity because the work will go on with increasing power after His death (14:12), greater in degree, not in quality, expand-

---

[1] Δεῖξον is more than argument; it is something visible. Ἀρκεῖ means "it is enough," the end of all doubt.

ing and extending over the world. They will have
direct access to Him in prayer, prayer to the Father and to the Son.[1] His " name " opens the door
to the Father's heart. " That will I do " (14: 14)
Jesus says, thus claiming power after His death on
a par with the Father. He means, of course, that
the requests are to be in accord with the Father's
will. The supreme test of love is obedience to the
commands of Jesus (14: 15).

He promises the presence of another Helper[2] to
take His place and to do for them what He has
been doing as Teacher and Guide (14: 16–26).
Jesus has been Advocate and Comforter while on
earth. He will continue to be our Advocate with
the Father (Rom. 8: 34; 1 John 2: 1), but the
Holy Spirit is God's Advocate with men (Rom.
8: 26 f.). His mission is to teach the disciples what
they need to know (14: 26). He is a Person[3] as is
the Father and the Son. The world cannot receive
the Holy Spirit (14: 17), this " spirit of truth," but
He will make His home in the believer's heart and
so bring Father and Son to us all as permanent
dwellers in our hearts (14: 17, 23; Matt. 28: 20).
This spiritual manifestation of Christ puzzles Judas

[1] This is true whether " me " is part of the text in verse
14 or not.

[2] ἄλλον. Another of same sort, not ἕτερον. παράκλητον
(our Paraclete) is the word for advocate or pleader. The
word is used for consoler or comforter.

[3] Note ἐκεῖνος in 14: 26, skipping the grammatical neuter
in πνεῦμα. We should say, " He," not " it " in speaking of
the Holy Spirit.

(not Iscariot), but it is gloriously true (14: 21 ff.). Jesus lives on forever and His eternal life beyond the grave is the guarantee of our life hereafter with Him (14: 19). At every turn we see Jesus saying things about Himself that only one conscious of equality with God could say unless, forsooth, Jesus is considered unbalanced in His intellect. He was so regarded by some of His enemies and, for a time, by His brothers, as we have seen, but the verdict of the world since has been that, if Jesus was crazy, it would be a good thing if the rest of the world could go crazy with Him. Paul was willing to be considered beside himself in his zeal for God (2 Cor. 5: 13). There are, indeed, a few wiseacre scholars, who to-day actually treat Jesus as a paranoiac,[1] though most men would call them the unbalanced faddists of over refinement of specialism. But the claim of Jesus has stood the test of time. The love for Jesus is what has lifted the world up towards God (14: 23) and it is doing it in spite of all the downward pull of the devil. As men are transformed by the love of Jesus, so do they approximate the ideal of God. Godlikeness is the goal of man.

Jesus leaves His peace with His disciples (14: 27–31), a legacy that the world cannot give and cannot take away. Jesus had won this peace of soul in the midst of conflict and it is possible for

[1] Cf. O. Holtzmann, " War Jesus Ekstatiker ? " (1903); Schaefer, " Jesus in psychiatrischer Beleuchtung " (1910); Werner, " Die psychische Gesundheit Jesu " (1908).

all to have the peace that passeth all understanding
(Phil. 4:7). A Christian may have it in the midst
of battle and in the presence of death. It is the
panacea for the troubled heart (John 14:27) and
should stop all nervous fluttering from fear.[1] Perfect love not only casts out fear (1 John 4:18), but
causes joy in its place (John 14:28). The day will
come when they will rejoice that Jesus has gone back
to the Father, gloomy as they are now. That day
did come when they had "great joy" after Jesus
ascended to the Father (Luke 24:52). Meanwhile
He faces the prince of this world who has no
sovereignty over Him (14:30). He arises with the
Eleven (14:31) who apparently go out and down
to the street and on towards Gethsemane in the
shadows caused by the passover moon.

Jesus continues His intimate talk and His plea
for their loyalty to Him. He gives them the
allegory of the vine and the branches (15:1–11).
Christ has cosmic relations with all men and with
the whole universe which trembles at His touch
(John 1:3; Rom. 8:22; Col. 1:15–20; Heb.
1:2). That idea is apparently presented here also
(John 15:2), but those who have spiritual life
through Him bear fruit (15:4) because the union is
vital and abiding (15:4–10). Jesus presses by repetition the "abiding" in Him. This will bring
fullness of joy to Christ and to the disciples (15:11).
Thus alone can the branch obtain life from the vine
and bear fruit which is the proof of life. This

[1] $\mu\eta\delta\grave{\epsilon}\ \delta\epsilon\iota\lambda\iota\acute{\alpha}\tau\omega.$

figure of the union of the believer with Christ is the same as that so common in Paul's Epistles when he constantly speaks of his being " in Christ." Jesus brings divine energy into our lives. If we let Him in, He brings life, peace, and power.

10. The Need for Mutual Love Between the Disciples (15 : 12–25).

Jesus has already spoken on this topic (13: 34 f.), but it will bear repetition. Jesus is offering the supreme proof of His love in laying down His life (15 : 13) for His friends (and for His enemies also). He asks for the same kind of devotion to Himself on the basis of friendship, for He has promoted them to this rank (15 : 15), but on the understanding that they prove worthy of the title by obedience to His commands (15 : 14). He chose them first (15 : 16) and has thus the right to make this mutual love a command (15 :16 f.). They must cling to each other against the world's hate which they are sure to get if they are at all like Jesus (15 : 18–21). Hatred of Jesus means hatred of the Father (15 : 23) for " now have they both seen and hated both me and my Father " (15 : 24). They have " seen " the Father in Christ, but did not recognize Him. But none the less they are without excuse (15 : 22, 24). It is as the Psalmist (Ps. 35 : 19; 69 : 4) said : " They hated me without a cause." It has literally been true that the world's hate has made Christians love each other better. Many a schism has been healed by the hand of a common persecution.

11. **The Help of the Paraclete** (15 : 26–16 : 15).

Jesus recurs to the coming of the Comforter
whom He will send from the Father (15 : 26) from
which statement is derived the doctrine of the Procession of the Holy Spirit and the Subordination
of the Spirit to the Father and the Son. There is
here a clear statement of the Persons in the Trinity,
not a mere modal Trinity. The Holy Spirit is to
bear witness about Jesus. He is the representative
of Christ upon earth, He and not the Pope or any
mere man. But the disciples must also bear witness of Jesus since they have been with Him since
the beginning of His ministry (15 : 27). They are
to witness even if they become martyrs [1] and are
put out of the synagogues and killed. Jesus now
speaks plainly and even chides them for no longer
asking " Whither goest thou ? " (16 : 5) as they did
in the beginning of this discourse (13 : 36). Even
Peter is quiet as they are all hushed into silence by
the wonder of Christ's words and the wealth of new
truths which He is now giving them. Jesus goes on
to explain that " it is expedient " [2] for them that
He go away, though they do not see it so. It is
very difficult to see things as they really are. We
have the short view and do not know the final outcome. The coming of the Comforter turns on the
going of Jesus (16 : 7). The point is that the Holy
Spirit is better qualified for the task of reaching the
hearts of men than is Jesus while in the flesh with

[1] Our " martyr " is simply the Greek μάρτυρ " witness."
[2] συμφέρει. Bears together for their good.

its necessary limitations of place. The Holy Spirit
has direct access to every man's heart. It is His
function to convict[1] the world. The world needs
its sin revealed to it. The sense of sin becomes
deadened so that people in decent society wink at
horrible vices till the conscience is aroused. Then
men crave again the ways of righteousness when
they face the terror of judgment. This lethargy
makes periodical revivals necessary. It took John
the Baptist to shake Judea and John Wesley to
quicken England and D. L. Moody to stir America
by the Spirit of God. The rejection of Jesus is sin
and leads to all possible sins (16 : 8–11). Jesus has
not told the disciples all that they need to know,
but all that they can bear now (16 : 12). The Spirit
of truth will guide[2] them into all the truth. Jesus
had claimed to be the embodiment of truth. Hence
He says of the Holy Spirit: " He shall glorify me:
for he shall take of mine,[3] and shall declare it unto
you" (16 : 14). That is the same as the Father's
store (16 : 15). Through the ages the Holy Spirit
guides men into " the mystery of God, even Christ,
in whom are all the treasures of wisdom and knowledge hidden" (Col. 2 : 3 f.). He has taught John
and Paul and He is ready to teach any of us who
will accept Him as Interpreter of Christ.

12. The Promise of Christ's Return (16 : 16–24).
The words of Jesus again puzzle the disciples as

---

[1] ἐλέγξει. Reprove at any rate and bring under conviction if possible.   [2] ὁδηγήσει. Lead the way as guide.
[3] ἐκ τοῦ ἐμοῦ. Out of my store.

He talks of their seeing Him again in " a little while,"
but they fear to question Him about it, for their
other questions revealed the depth of their ignorance. Nothing is so illuminating as questions.
If listeners could only ask the preacher some questions as he preaches, he could see how far he may
be missing his goal. Jesus notes their silence and
explains His enigmatic saying and points to the
day when there will be no need to ask further questions, when all will be clear. Meanwhile they can
ask the Father in His name all that they wish to
know and that they ought to know. Jesus apparently has in mind the Second Coming and the
Judgment, though He may also include by the
" little while " His resurrection. But they must
learn to suffer and to wait, for sorrow shall be
turned into joy.

13. The Certainty of Victory (16 : 25-33).

Jesus admits that He has spoken to them " in
dark sayings " [1] (16 : 25), but it was a necessity.
Language after all is symbolic and pictographic.
Perfect understanding can get beyond the need of
speech. Jesus promises a day when He can speak
" openly " [2] to them without " dark sayings." So
Jesus tries it now and says in so many words that
He is going back to the Father from whom He
came into the world.[3] At last the disciples see a

[1] ἐν παροιμίαις.

[2] παρρησία. A full story, nothing held back.

[3] The use of κόσμος is one of the characteristic words of
this Gospel. It occurs in various senses.

gleam of light: " Lo, now speakest thou plainly,
and speakest no dark saying" (16 : 29). " Now
know we," they go on, as if they have made the
great discovery, " that thou knowest all things and
needest not that any man should ask thee: by
this we believe that thou camest forth from God "
(16 : 30). They had accepted Him as Messiah at
the start (1 : 41), but they had not comprehended
that He was God manifest in the flesh even when
they used the term " the Son of God " (1 : 49).
Slowly these men have been led to see that the
Father and the Son are one in nature and ought to
be ready now for the departure of Jesus and the
tutelage of the Holy Spirit. But, alas, their confidence is premature, for Jesus says : " Do ye now [1]
believe?" (16 : 31). He had urged faith in Himself as in God (14 : 1). This they now claim, but
Jesus reminds them of their desertion this very
night: " Ye shall be scattered, every man to his
own; and shall leave me alone: and yet I am not
alone, because the Father is with me " (16 : 32).
With God He has already won the victory for
Himself and for them : " In the world ye have
tribulation : but be of good cheer [2]; I have over-
come [3] the world " (16 : 33).

14. The Prayer of Consecration [4] (17).
This is the real Lord's Prayer, His own plea at

---

[1] ἄρτι. At this juncture.   [2] θαρσεῖτε. Good courage.
[3] νενίκηκα. State of completion by anticipation.
[4] This is Westcott's phrase, but I had fallen upon it before
consulting his great work.

this supreme crisis of His ministry. Further talk
to the disciples is useless, as they have already
heard more than they can digest. Jesus probably
pauses near the eastern gate of the city by the
Temple [1] and prays " lifting up his eyes to heaven "
(17 : 1) in audible voice so that the disciples hear.
Westcott calls this prayer " at once a prayer and a
profession and a revelation," " the consummation
of the glory of God through Christ, the Word Incarnate, from stage to stage, issuing in a perfect
unity." The prayer falls into three obvious parts :
(1) For Himself, 1–5. (2) For the Eleven Apostles,
6–19. (3) For All Believers of All Time, 20–26.
There is thought enough in this prayer for a volume of exposition. Jesus begins with " Father"
and " thy Son," but soon (verse 4) says " thee "
and " me." " The hour " [2] is used in various senses
by Jesus concerning His work. It was once the
public entrance upon His Messianic ministry (John
2 : 4), while it is here the hour of consummation which
" has arrived." [3] The glorifying of the Son and the
Father (cf. 13 : 31 f.) is more than victory over
death and includes the resurrection and ascension.
The mission of the Son is to bring salvation (eternal
life) to men who believe and Jesus possesses the
authority (or power) [4] over all flesh as the Head of

---

[1] Westcott feels certain that this prayer was uttered in the
Temple courts.   That is quite possible.

[2] ἡ ὥρα.

[3] ἐλήλυθεν.   The entrance upon the hour has come, not
the completion of it.   [4] ἐξουσία.

humanity (17 : 2). Eternal life is described as the knowledge [1] of God and Christ (17 : 3).[2] Jesus is conscious of having finished His work, a victorious work, the task given Him by the Father (17 : 4). Hence He longs for the restoration of the glory which He had with the Father in the preincarnate state (17 : 5. Cf. 1 : 1). There is here consciousness of equality and fellowship with God.

Jesus had come to earth to " manifest " God (cf. 1 : 18) and He began with the Twelve Apostles as the nucleus. He claims success with these men in spite of the case of Judas, " the son of perdition," [3] whose fate fulfills Scripture (Ps. 12 : 9) and whose character was known to Jesus from the start (6 : 70 f.). The devil had him all the while, and Jesus " kept " and " guarded " [4] (7 : 12) them in the garrison of jealous love (cf. Phil. 4 : 7). They needed the anxious watch-care of Jesus and He is profoundly concerned for their welfare now that He is going to leave them. He is not here praying for the world, but for these eleven men (17 : 9), though He does elsewhere for the unsaved (Luke 23 : 34). Jesus has faithfully given these men God's word and He prays that they may be sanctified [5] in its truth

---

[1] γινώσκωσιν. Experimental knowledge and continuous experience. Linear present.

[2] Westcott doubts if the words " Jesus Christ " were spoken by Jesus in the prayer and considers them a parenthetical addition by the writer.

[3] ὁ υἱὸς τῆς ἀπωλείας. Destined for perdition.

[4] ἐτήρουν (continuous, imperfect) and ἐφύλαξα (constative aorist).   [5] ἁγίασον. Set apart to and in the truth.

(17 : 17). These men are not to be spiritual re-
cluses out of the world. They are to fight on in
the world, different from the world, in it and not of
it, to transform the world, to rescue it from the
prince of the world, and bring it to the feet of
Jesus (17 : 15-19). They are Christ's missionaries
into the world as Christ is God's Apostle [1] to earth
(17 : 18 f.).

But all Christians are to be apostles (missionaries)
in this sense. They are to pass on the word of
truth and of life through the ages. For these mes-
sengers of truth Jesus prays. The item that is uppermost in Christ's heart as He faces the future is
the need of unity on the part of His followers,
" that they may all be one." [2]   Jesus had just prayed
for unity among the Eleven (17 : 11). They had
shown a lack of love on this very night in the strife
for primacy at the passover meal. There is abundant room for anxiety about the future believers.
After conversion men still have the same psycho-
logical traits and characteristics. Jesus is not here
praying specifically for organic union. That was a
reality already and continued so for a long time.
The schism which Jesus fears is a deeper and more
serious one than that and the usual precursor to
division. It is the jealousy that makes coöperation
difficult or impossible. The most important question before Christians to-day is not organic union.
That is folly without harmony of conviction and
feeling and cannot be forced by mechanical efforts,

----

[1] ἀπέστειλας.   [2] ἵνα πάντες ἓν ὧσιν (17 : 21).

however desirable in the abstract.   Lack of unity is a much more serious matter than lack of union. This lack of unity appears in the members of the same denomination, yea, of the same local church. This is what disturbs the heart of Christ.   He pleads and prays for a unity, a oneness of spirit, like that between Himself and the Father.   In that case schism is impossible.   The world will then come to know God in Christ.   But Jesus knows the Father even if the world does not.   He has revealed the Father to the world (17 : 25 f.).

V

THE SCORN OF CHRIST'S ENEMIES
(Chapters 18 and 19)
" Behold, the Man."

1. Into Gethsemane (18 : 1).

JESUS " went forth over the brook Kidron, where was a garden, into which he entered, himself and his disciples " (18 : 1). He went forth from the place where He had been praying, went on through the gate, and down into the valley, the disciples full of troubled thoughts. John's Gospel omits all reference to the institution of the Lord's Supper at the close of the passover meal (Matt. 26 : 26–29 ; Mark 14 : 22–25 ; Luke 22 : 17–20 ; 1 Cor. 11 : 23–26) and before the discourse and prayer given in John 14–17, Luke (22 : 39) notes that it was the " custom " of Jesus to go to the Mount of Olives and Matthew (26 : 36) and Mark (14 : 32) identify this place of prayer as Gethsemane. John omits also the narrative of the Agony in the garden, but adds (18 : 2) that Judas knew the place whither Jesus was in the habit of going in the night to pray.

2. The Betrayal and Arrest of Jesus (18 : 2–10).
John emphasizes the fact that Judas took ad-

vantage of his knowledge of Jesus' habits[1] in prayer
to betray Him. But even so he comes not only
with police officers[2] from the Sanhedrin (chief
priests and Pharisees), but also with " the band "[3]
of Roman soldiers (18 : 3) from the garrison in the
tower of Antonia, a revelation of Jewish fear of
Jesus. They may (Dods, *in loco*) have dreaded a
popular uprising after the arrest (cf. 7 : 32–49;
12 : 42). This band of soldiers had " weapons."[4]
They also had " lanterns and torches."[5] It was
full moon, but it may have been cloudy and there
would be shadows from the olive trees in the garden.
So the conspirators would take no chances of
failure. John (18 : 4) comments on the fact that
Jesus is fully aware of the plans of His enemies :
" knowing all things that were coming upon him."
This is fully shown in the Synoptic account of the
Agony as Jesus arises to meet the betrayer (Mark
14 : 42) and John also (13 : 27) tells of Christ's command to Judas. So Jesus steps forth out of the
enclosure to meet the party coming to arrest Him
and boldly challenges them (18 : 4). He avows His
identity and exerts His power over the company in

---

[1] πολλάκις συνήχθη. Constative aorist.

[2] ὑπηρέτας. Cf. John 7 : 32.

[3] τὴν σπεῖραν. Probably not the full cohort, but a de-
tachment only. Polybius (XI. 23) uses σπεῖρα for the Latin
manipulus, two hundred men.

[4] ὅπλων. Probably swords and slings.

[5] μετὰ φανῶν καὶ λαμπάδων. In Dion. Hal. XI. 5 we
read : " The soldiers rushed out of their tents with lanterns
and torches."

a marvellous manner. They not simply went backward, but " fell to the ground " (18 : 6). Thus He proved His mastery over His enemies and showed to Judas and the rest that He gave Himself up voluntarily, not because they came against Him with armed soldiers. This episode must have staggered Judas a bit, but he was too deep in the mire to draw back now. John does not mention the despicable kiss of Judas, the sign to his companions. It was not really needed, though carried out, since Jesus confessed His identity and made a plea for the freedom of the Eleven (18 : 8). They had no trouble in seizing and binding Jesus as was customary with dangerous criminals (18 : 12). The chief captain [1] or military tribune had actually come along. The Sadducees had represented Jesus as an enemy of public order (Westcott, *in loco*). Simon Peter could stand this procedure no longer and made use of one of the two swords (Luke 22 : 38) that they happened to have with them, in an effort to cut off the head of Malchus, servant of the high priest. But he only got his right ear (John 18 : 10), probably because Malchus dodged. Jesus healed the ear (Luke 22 : 51) and bade Peter put up his sword (John 18 : 11), adding with the calmness won through His Agony, " The cup that my Father hath given me, shall I not drink it ? " So it was all over. Jesus not only would not resist arrest, He would not even allow His disciples to fight for Him. " They that take the sword shall perish with

[1] χιλίαρχος. Leader of a cohort.

the sword" (Matt. 26 : 52), as all the world is now seeing. Jesus had twelve legions of angels at His command if He wished to use them (Matt. 26 : 53). The death of Jesus is thus shown to be voluntary as it had to be to possess moral value for our sins. But the effect on the disciples was disastrous, for they all fled in terror to save themselves from a like fate. It was indeed the hour and the power of darkness (Luke 22 : 53).

3. Jesus Before Annas (18 : 13–14, 19–23).

John alone records this preliminary examination of Jesus by Annas preceding the appearance before the Sanhedrin. He says "first" with an allusion to the examination before Caiaphas. Probably the reason was simply to keep Jesus in a secure place while the Sanhedrin were assembling for the trial. It was, besides, a mark of respect to this powerful ex-high priest, the head of the Sadducees. Annas had been high priest himself[1] A. D. 7–14 and he kept the office in the family till five successive sons held it besides his son-in-law Joseph Caiaphas who now has it (A. D. 18–36).

The Talmud[2] pronounces a curse on "the family of Hanan and their serpent-hissings," and yet at this time Annas (Hanan) had a powerful following. The Talmud, besides, gives the Pharisaic standpoint against the Sadducees. John alone explains that Annas is the father-in-law of Caiaphas. This fact makes it clear how Annas has so much power,

[1] Josephus, "*Ant.*," *XVIII*. ii. 1 f.   [2] *Pesach.*, 57 *a*.

though not in office. Annas is probably the moving spirit in the whole business (Westcott), certainly from the standpoint of the Sadducees.

It is not clear why Caiaphas (18:19) questions Jesus in this informal examination before Annas. It is possible that John may here refer to Annas by "high priest" out of courtesy, as popular usage uses the title "governor" after a man is no longer occupying that position. Verse 24 seems to make it plain that Jesus is still before Annas in verses 19–23.[1] The question to Jesus about His disciples and His teaching was keenly resented by the Master who ignores the implied slur upon His disciples as the ignorant multitude (cf. 7:49). As to the teaching of Jesus, that is public property (18:20 f.), as Annas knows only too well by personal experience (cf. Matt. 21:23–23:39). The question implied that there was something secret and sinister in His teaching which He was not willing to tell in public. Socrates[2] says when on trial: "If any one says that he has ever learned or heard anything from me in private which the world has not heard, be assured he says what is not true." Jesus did teach the Eleven many things that He did not proclaim to the world, but nothing contradictory to His public teaching and only to make them effective teachers of the public. His teaching was not eso-

---

[1] However, ἀπέστειλεν in verse 24 can have the force in English of a past-perfect. That is, it may merely refer to what had already taken place. The Greeks did not usually draw distinctions in past time.   [2] Plato, "Apology 33."

teric in the usual sense of the word. His protest
was met with a "slap"[1] of the hand by one of the
officers, which Jesus did not return (could not, in
fact, if still bound, as was unlikely, but would not
in any case), though He made further protest
against this abuse of His person and of His rights
to a fair trial[2] (18 : 22 f.). He did not turn the
other cheek, showing that His language on that
subject (Matt. 5 : 39) is not to be taken too literally.

4. Peter's Downfall (18 : 15–18, 25–27).

All the Gospels tell this sad story, giving three
denials, but in varying order. It is not possible
to relate them clearly to the examination before
Annas and Caiaphas. They covered some time,
since Luke (22 : 59) notes an hour between the
second and the third denial. Peter and John rallied
from their flight and fright first of the Eleven and
followed Jesus on to the house of the high priest
Caiaphas (John 18 : 15), but Peter " afar off" (Mark
14 : 54). John, that " other disciple" " known to
the high priest,"[3] " entered with Jesus into the
court[4] of the high priest." It is quite possible that
Annas also had rooms in the house of Caiaphas.

---

[1] ῥάπισμα.

[2] The conditions (εἰ and the indicative) in verse 23 are of
the first class and assume, for the sake of argument, the truth
of the condition.

[3] γνωστὸς τῷ ἀρχιερεῖ. How he won this acquaintance we
do not know.

[4] The αὐλή was originally the quadrangle around which
the house was built, but it came to be used for the house
itself.

If so, the denials of Peter were in this building where both Annas and Caiaphas lived and John and the Synoptists do not disagree as to the place. The case of Peter is almost tragic. He had tried to kill a man in defence of Jesus and then fled in spite of his boast. He came back, but followed afar off. He lingers at the door outside,[1] unable to get in till John, " the other disciple the acquaintance of the high priest " (note the circumlocution to avoid his name), went out and spoke to " the portress "[2] (18: 16). This maid, knowing John and letting Peter in at his request, had good reason to suspect Peter's connection with Jesus. Her question politely expects the answer " No,"[3] though she thought " Yes," and had a decided " fling " at Jesus in " this man "[4] (18: 17). Caught off his guard and helped on by the very form of the maid's question and his desire for secrecy, he said the fatal words of denial. Inside the quadrangle the servants and the officers, who had helped arrest Jesus, were warming themselves by the fire which they had made, for it was cold. Twice John notes (18: 18, 25) that Peter was also warming himself.[5] Again on a general accusation he denied being a disciple of Jesus. The Synoptics reverse the order of these

---

[1] πρὸς τῇ θύρᾳ ἔξω.

[2] τῇ θυρωρῷ. See interesting article on " Peter's Denials," in particular re " the portress," by Sir W. M. Ramsay, in *The Expository Times* for 1916.   [3] μή.

[4] τοῦ ἀνθρώπου τούτου. This fellow in contempt.

[5] θερμαινόμενος. Direct middle.

two denials, but all agree in the order of the third
and climacteric one. Mark speaks of the cock
crowing at this juncture (Mark 14:68). Probably
Peter hid himself for an hour, but could not stay
away, for yonder was Jesus on trial in the room
above the quadrangle where the Sanhedrin sat.
John had gone on into the room. So Peter came
back and one after another, men and maids, charged
him with being a Galilean as shown by his speech
(Matt. 26:73). But it was the sharp, close query of a
kinsman of Malchus: "Did not I see thee in the garden
with him?" (John 18:26) that threw Peter completely
off his balance. He "lost his temper," as we say,
and cursed and swore to prove his lack of acquaintance with Jesus. The cock crew the second time
(Mark 14:72). Jesus turned and looked at Peter
(Luke 22:61) and Peter remembered the word of
Jesus and went out with a broken heart, weeping
bitterly. But it was done. It is not hard to see
the steps in his downfall. They are plain enough, as
are the steps down-hill which any disciple may take.
Judas has betrayed Jesus. Peter has denied Him.
The devil is sifting them all. John alone is now
with Jesus. But Jesus stands before His accusers
undaunted in spite of this added blow from Simon
Peter, His trusted lieutenant.

5. Jesus Before Caiaphas (18:24).

The supplementary character of the Fourth Gospel is again illustrated at this point. He gives no
details at all of the trial before Caiaphas and the

Sanhedrin and merely alludes to the fact as if to refer his readers to the Synoptic Gospels for the story of this phase of the subject. All that is here taken for granted. Indeed, but for Matthew (27 : 1 f.) and Mark (15 : 1) we should not know that there were two hearings before the Sanhedrin, one at night when the real examination took place (Matt. 26: 57, 59, 60–68; Mark 14: 53, 55–65), the other after dawn to ratify the illegal decision already reached. Luke gives only this phase of the trial (22: 66–23: 1). The only item in John's one sentence to note is that Jesus is said to have been " bound " again before being sent to Caiaphas. This implies that He was set free during the hearing before Annas.

6. Jesus Before Pilate (18 : 28–19 : 16).

Here John has more to tell and most of it is new. Pilate is in his official residence, the Prætorium.[1] It was probably in the tower of Antonia and not the palace of Herod. John draws the picture with characteristic vividness. It is " early," between " dawn " (Luke 22 : 66) and sunrise (John 19 : 14). The accusers are in a great hurry to get the business through before the populace begin to stir. When they find Jesus a condemned criminal in the eyes of Roman law, besides the condemnation of the Sanhedrin, the halo will drop from the brow of the

---

[1] τὸ πραιτώριον. The technical sense in the provinces (cf. Acts 23 : 35), but not that at Rome (cf. Phil. 1 : 13). It was originally " the general's tent."

Nazarene in the eyes of these Galileans who so recently hailed Him as Messiah in the very faces of the Sanhedrin in the Temple. It is all well planned and is moving on with expedition. And yet the conspirators will not enter the Prætorium, for that is a Gentile's house. They wish to keep on celebrating the passover which has already begun.[1] So the accusers stood outside till Pilate " went forth " (John 18 : 29) to ask for their charge against Jesus. John does not give the charges, but only the haughty assumption [2] of infallibility on the part of the Sanhedrin, though they say nothing of their own trial when Pilate offers to turn Jesus over to them (18 : 30 f.). The reason is that they wish the death of Jesus and their previous condemnation is futile because they do not at this time possess the power of life and death. They probably here brought forward the accusations against Jesus mentioned in Luke 23 : 2, but with no allusion to what they had done, least of all did they tell how they had finally gotten the charge of blasphemy. John's narrative evidently has in mind Luke's account, for the question of Pilate to Jesus whom he now takes back into the Prætorium shows that He has been charged with claiming to be King (John 18 : 33). It was a charge

[1] So I interpret this disputed phrase to " eat the passover." See my discussion of it on page 256 of Broadus' " Harmony of the Gospels." John uses " passover " elsewhere, always for the whole feast. In 2 Chron. 30 : 22 we note that " they did eat the festival seven days."

[2] The term κακοποιός (here κακὸν ποιῶν) evil-doer occurs in Polybius and 1 Peter.

that Pilate could not ignore, without peril of arraign-
ment before Cæsar, who would brook no rival.   This
conversation between Pilate and Jesus is one of the
striking things in John's Gospel.   The question of
Jesus to Pilate (John 18 : 34) is pertinent, for Jesus
does claim to be the King Messiah in the Kingdom
of God, but not a political king as the Pharisees
wished Him to be and now mean to charge Him
with claiming to be when He said He was " Christ
a King " (Luke 23 : 2).   But Pilate is indignant at
the suggestion that he cares for the Jewish theological refinements.[1]   " Am I a Jew ? " he fairly blurts
out as he demands the nature of the crime of Jesus
(John 18 : 35).   The reply of Jesus puzzled Pilate
more than ever.   The two men lived in different
mental worlds.   Pilate could not comprehend the
language of Canaan.   This kingdom " not of this
world " was beyond his ken.   Alas, one must add,
many of the followers of Jesus have forgotten these
words (18 : 36), for religious wars between Christians
have not been uncommon.   Pilate presses the point
a bit further and Jesus confesses to being a King
who bears witness concerning the truth (18 : 37).
At this Pilate sees a gleam of light, for after all
" what is truth ? "[2]   Truth stood before Pilate
and he did not know what sort of a thing truth
was.   " I am the truth."   There is a famous ana-
gram on this question : " Quid est veritas ? "   Trans-
posing the letters makes " Est vir qui adest."   But

[1] Cf. Gallio's scorn in Acts 18 : 14 f.
[2] τί ἐστιν ἀλήθεια.

Pilate was no philosopher and no theologian. He was merely a practical politician and he was sure that the realm of truth in which Christ is King in no way conflicts with the territory over which Cæsar rules. So he makes up his mind that he is dealing with a mystic dreamer, perhaps a bit unbalanced, but certainly harmless. He openly avows his belief in the innocence of Jesus to the utter chagrin of the Sanhedrin (18 : 38). When he proposes that he release unto them " the King of the Jews," according to his custom to set one prisoner free at the feast, with a playful turn to the title and their charge, he is surprised at their choice of Barabbas, a real criminal at the head of an insurrection, perhaps a zealot and a sort of national hero, though an outlaw (18 : 40). John does not follow all the ins and outs of the trial before Pilate nor the fiasco before Herod (Luke 23 : 6–12). But he adds details about the end of the matter. Pilate had Jesus scourged[1] to see if that would pacify the Jewish leaders, but it was useless. The appearance of Jesus in a purple robe and a crown of thorns upon His brow and the half humorous sally of Pilate : " Behold, the man ! "[2] (18 : 5) even after his explicit statement of the innocence of Jesus (18 : 4) availed nothing with the people. They were in no mood for humour. They wanted the blood of Jesus and would be satisfied with nothing less. The effect was simply to make the leaders raise the cry " Crucify him, crucify

[1] ἐμαστίγωσεν. Causative action.
[2] ʼΙδοὺ ὁ ἄνθρωπος. Behold, the fellow !

him." [1] Crucifixion was not a Jewish mode of pun-
ishment, though Alexander Jannæus used it upon
eight hundred Pharisees, copying the habits of the
Hellenes. But the Romans used it constantly for
criminals on Golgotha and the Jews will be only too
glad to see Jesus crucified. In a pet Pilate yields to
the Jews and bids them to take Him and crucify
Him, "for I find no crime in him" (18 : 6), the
most astonishing decision ever rendered by a judge,
a frank yielding to popular clamour in the face of
the acknowledged evidence and all justice, a sentence
that brands Pilate forever as a coward and makes
his name a byword through the centuries. But the
Jewish leaders in their glee over their triumph tell
too much: "We have a law, and by that law he
ought to die, because he made himself the Son of
God" (18 : 7). When He was put on oath by
Caiaphas contrary to law, Jesus had confessed to
this claim before the Sanhedrin (Matt. 26 : 63–66)
and on His confession they had passed sentence of
death which Pilate now unwittingly confirms. But
the words "the Son of God" in connection with
Pilate's strange interview with Jesus and his wife's
dream (Matt. 27 : 19) made him more superstitious
and afraid than ever (John 19 : 8). So, in spite
of his surrender, Pilate takes Jesus back into the
Prætorium for a further interview. He affects indignation at Jesus, but is really overawed by the
tone of authority in Him (19 : 10 f.). The result is
that Pilate makes one more feeble effort to release

[1] Σταύρωσον, σταύρωσον.

the prisoner, whereupon the Jews threaten to report
Pilate to Cæsar as harbouring a rival and so being
guilty of treason (19 : 12). He knew all the time
that they would do this and his vacillation is thus
explained. He made another presentation of Jesus
with the salutation : " Behold, your King." " Shall
I crucify your King?" he urges as he sat on the
judgment seat[1] on the elevated stone pavement[2]
(Gabbatha in Hebrew) in front of the Prætorium.
The Sadducees (chief priests) retort: " We have no
king but Cæsar," and swallow all their pride and all
their hate of Rome to compass the death of Jesus
(19 : 13–16). It is clear that the claim of Jesus to
be the Messiah, the Son of God, the King, not of
the Jews, but of Israel, is the *crux* of the charges
against Him. He will not, He cannot deny His
divine Sonship and His Messianic mission. Pilate,
cowardly as he undoubtedly was, yet had a Roman's
sense of justice and felt that a stupendous wrong was
done to an innocent man which he did not have the
courage to prevent. His spectacular washing of his
hands simply emphasized the situation and his un-
easy conscience made him protest that all the guilt
was upon the Jews. But unfortunately there is
guilt enough for all and he bears his share along
with Judas, Annas, Caiaphas, the Sanhedrin, and all
who clamoured for the blood of Jesus to come upon
their heads and upon their children (Matt. 27 : 24 f.).
The impossible thing has happened. The one Perfect Man of all the ages is under condemnation to

[1] βήματος.　　[2] λιθόστρωτον. Tessellated pavement.

die at the hands of the Chosen People of God and against the forms of their own and Roman law. The Jews are guilty of treason to their true King and Pilate of treason to his office (Westcott). The Hope of the Messiah had cheered the Jews through the ages and now they have compassed His death in a resentful mood that reveals their own spiritual deficiency in the supreme crisis of history.[1]

7. Jesus on the Cross (19 : 17–37).

John omits the mockery of Jesus by the soldiers (Matt. 27 : 27–30) after the sentence. Three hours elapsed between the sentence by Pilate at 6 A. M., Roman time (John 19 : 14) and the beginning of the Crucifixion at 9 A. M. (third hour Jewish time) (Mark 15 : 25). John notes that the Jewish authorities " received "[2] Jesus from Pilate though they had the Roman soldiers as their instruments (19 : 23). Westcott pertinently remarks that they received Him for execution when they would not have Him as Redeemer (1 : 11).[3] John gives no details of the *Via Dolorosa* to the Cross save the one item : " bearing the cross for himself" (19 : 17). So He began the mournful way like any common criminal, carrying His own cross literally as He had taught the disciples to do daily (Luke 9 : 23 f.). This in no way contradicts the Synoptic account of the enforced (Mark 15 : 21)

---

[1] See Innes, " The Trial of Jesus " (1899) ; Stalker, " The Trial and Death of Jesus Christ " (1894).

[2] παρέλαβον. [3] οὐ παρέλαβον.

service of Simon of Cyrene which may have been
due to the exhaustion of Jesus, a theory supported
also (Westcott) by the words used in Mark 15 : 22 :
" They bring him."   The place of a skull (Golgotha)
was probably the knoll to the north of the city with
two hollow caves in its face, thus roughly resem-
bling a huge skull.   Crucifixions took place outside of the city, though near (John 19 : 19) and
this place, Calvaria, and not the Church of the
Holy Sepulchre inside the walls, is the true site of
the Crucifixion of Jesus.   John simply mentions
" two others " [1] between whom Jesus is crucified,
probably on the very cross designed for Barabbas,
the leader with these two " robbers " [2] (Matt. 27 : 38 ;
Mark 15 : 27) of a large band of insurrectionists
(possibly zealots).   John gives more in detail the
placing of the title on the cross which Pilate wrote.
Probably the full title was : " This is Jesus of Nazareth the King of the Jews."   Thus Pilate correctly
presents the name, residence, and crime of the
victim.   It was written in Latin as the legal form,
in Hebrew (Aramaic) for the ordinary Palestinian
Jews, in Greek for Hellenistic Jews and the public
generally, since Greek was the current language of
the world (19 : 20).   On the Cross of Jesus thus
meet the three chief civilizations of the world
(Roman law, Greek culture, Hebrew religion).   The
Jewish leaders greatly disliked the form of Pilate's

---

[1] ἄλλους δύο.

[2] Λῃσταί. Highway robbers, bandits, not petty thieves.
Luke (23 : 33) only calls them " malefactors " κακοῦργοι.

superscription, for they at bottom had national hopes of a Messiah, but Pilate was stubborn at last on this technicality after his abject surrender on the main issue (19 : 21 f.) like many another weak man.

John likewise gives a full account of the casting of lots by the four soldiers for the seamless coat or tunic[1] of Jesus after dividing equally His other garments[2] (19 : 23 f.). The soldiers, of course, have no thought of fulfilling Scripture (Ps. 22 : 18) in so doing.

The scene between Jesus and His mother is given only by John (19 : 25-27). He contrasts[3] the soldiers with the group of women standing by[4] the Cross of Christ. There seem to be four women in the group —Mary the mother of Jesus, Salome the mother of the sons of Zebedee (cf. John 19 : 25 ; Mark 15 : 40 ; Matt. 27 : 56), Mary the wife of Clopas (mother of James the less and Joses, Matt. 27 : 56 ; Mark 15 : 40), and Mary Magdalene. The women are true, as one would expect, in an hour like this, whatever is the conduct of the men. The sword has pierced the soul of Mary, the mother of Jesus, as Simeon had said it would (Luke 2 : 35), but she did not flinch nor was she ashamed to own Jesus when the rulers have rejected Him. Once a cloud of doubt did gather over her faith, but she was true, though she could not reconcile this outcome with the word of the Angel Gabriel. The Beloved

---

[1] χιτών. The inner garment.
[2] μέρη (head-dress, sandals, girdle, outer garment or ἱμάτιον). [3] μὲν—δὲ. [4] παρά. By the side of.

Disciple, who we have taken to be the Apostle
John, the author of the Gospel, is also there, the
only one of the Apostles who came.   It is a tender
human touch in this Gospel when Jesus speaks from
the Cross to His mother and to John and commends
them as mother and son, titles of loving respect.
John accepted the precious charge " from that
hour " and probably took Mary to his lodging [1] at
once, though it does not follow (Westcott) that he
had a permanent home in Jerusalem at this time.
Legend has it that they lived together in Jerusalem
eleven years, when Mary died, and then again that
she lived with John in Ephesus years afterwards, but
we know nothing.   It was clearly impossible for
Jesus to commend His mother to His own brothers,
for they as yet disbelieved in Him.

John passes by the three hours of darkness
(twelve to three), but gives two sayings at the end
(19 : 28–30).   He emphasizes the fact of the consciousness [2] of Jesus to the end.   He had refused
the stupefying drinks twice offered Him according
to the custom of the times, but He does take a sip
of the stimulating vinegar at the last which is offered
upon His cry: " I thirst."   This cry of physical
anguish is wrung from Jesus by the intolerable
thirst, the severest pang connected with the slow
crucifixion.   The outcry fulfilled a Messianic Psalm
(69 : 21), and shows that the Messiah suffered to the
uttermost.   The other cry is one of victory : " It is

[1] εἰς τὰ ἴδια.   So used in the papyri.
[2] εἰδώς.

finished." [1] This He knew was to be the outcome of His atoning death. The work of redemption is now uppermost in the mind of the Saviour as He dies on the Cross, the victim of human hate and for human sin. No theory of the atonement can present all the truth in this stupendous tragedy. But it is certainly the voluntary giving of His blood for our sin by the one perfect and sinless man who is also the Son of God. It is a substitutionary death, but it has moral value because of the character of Jesus and His spirit in offering Himself for us. Here is the core of the Gospel as Jesus conceived it and His biographers have interpreted it. He gave up His spirit to death in order thus to triumph over death and sin. The simple grandeur of John's words passes all comment as the death of Jesus on the Cross is the culmination of human history, the ground of hope for the race.

John alone (19 : 31–37) gives the story of the breaking of the legs (*crurifragium*) of the two robbers by the soldiers at the request of the Jews (19 : 31) so that the bodies could be taken down before the Sabbath began at sunset (six o'clock). The bodies were to come down by night anyhow, but the approach of the Sabbath made the Jewish leaders very sensitive on the subject. The Gospels all (Matt. 27 : 62; Mark 15 : 42; Luke 23 : 54; John 19 : 31) explain that the day of the crucifixion

---

[1] τετέλεσται. Finished to stay finished. Done once for all.

is the " Preparation,"[1] that is the day before the
Sabbath. This Sabbath was a " high "[2] day because it was also in the passover week. But the
legs of Jesus were not broken because it was not
necessary. He was already dead when the soldiers
came. To make sure, however, one of the soldiers
pierced the side of Jesus, from which " there came
out blood and water." This astonishing circumstance is certified to by the writer of the Gospel
who claims to speak as an eye-witness to the occur-
rence. He reiterates that he knows[3] that he is
speaking the truth and wishes to induce belief in
his statement. He sees the fulfillment of Scripture
(Ps. 34 : 20; Zech. 12 : 10), but he has another
purpose. The Docetic Gnostics denied the real
humanity of Jesus. So John takes pains to bear
witness to the fact of seeing blood come out of the
side of Jesus to show the reality of the human
nature of Christ. The credibility of such an oc-
currence is vouched for by modern medical science[4] on the theory of a rupture of the blood ves-
sels of the heart as the cause of death. Literally,
therefore, Jesus died of a broken heart, broken by
the sin of the world (John 1 : 29; 2 Cor. 5 : 21) as
He suffered alone in the darkness (Matt. 27 : 46).[5]

---

[1] παρασκευή. The name to-day for Friday in modern
Greek.   [2] μεγάλη.

[3] ἐκεῖνος οἶδεν. Not God knows, but ὁ ἑωρακὼς knows.

[4] Dr. Stroud, " Physical Causes of the Death of Christ."

[5] See Clow, " In the Day of the Cross " (1909); Denney, " The Death of Christ " (2d ed., 1911); Forsyth,
" The Cruciality of the Cross" (1909); Ross, " The

8. Jesus in the Tomb (19 : 38–42).

The Gospels all tell of the kindly love of Joseph of Arimathea who boldly (Mark 15 : 43) avowed his secret faith in Jesus (John 19 : 38), no longer afraid of the Jews though a member of the Sanhedrin (Luke 23 : 50 f.) who had not consented to their purposes about Jesus. Perhaps he was not invited or refused to go to that meeting. He was rich (Matt. 27 : 57) and was looking for the Kingdom of God (Luke 23 : 51). Timid people are often emboldened by catastrophes. Pilate expresses surprise that Jesus is already dead when Joseph asks for His body (Mark 15 : 44). An avaricious governor could sell the privilege of burial in such cases, but Pilate chose to be gracious to Joseph. Friends took the body of the Baptist (Matt. 15 : 12) and of Stephen (Acts 8 : 2) for decent burial. John alone records the courage of Nicodemus, another secret disciple and member of the Sanhedrin who had also opposed their schemes against Jesus (7 : 50). He was emboldened by the example of Joseph and furnished a hundred pounds of myrrh and aloes, a costly gift to cover the body of Jesus with these aromatics as we do with flowers. So these two members of the Sanhedrin, the body that had compassed the death of Jesus, give His body proper burial according to the custom of the Jews, with the linen clothes and the spices. The forms were duly observed by these two men who in

Cross " (1912) ; Stalker, " The Trial and Death of Jesus Christ " (1894).

the late afternoon of Friday lay the body of Jesus in Joseph's new [1] tomb, freshly cut in the rock in the garden near the scene of the crucifixion on Golgotha Hill. There " they laid Jesus " [2] reverently, if a bit hastily, for the day was swiftly dying and the Sabbath drew on at sunset, the dawn of the Jewish twenty-four hour day (Luke 23 : 54). There John leaves the dead Christ. He does not tell of the watching, wistful women, nor of the feverish Pharisees who have a Roman guard placed by the tomb with a seal of state upon it to keep Jesus in the grave (Matt. 27 : 62–66). The Apostles were not at the burial, so it seems, nor the women. The hearts of all were broken and bleeding. They had followed Jesus through the years with mounting hopes and now their Hope lay buried in Joseph's tomb. Our own hearts are torn as we read the story now. What must it have been for those in the valley of the shadow of this death ?

[1] καινόν, not νέον.　　　　[2] ἔθηκαν τὸν Ἰησοῦν.

VI

THE VINDICATION

(Chapters 20 and 21)

" *My Lord and my God.*"

THE resurrection of Jesus from the grave is the basal fact in the revival of hope in the disciples and on this fact rests the claim of Jesus to be the Messiah and Saviour. He had repeatedly foretold His resurrection on the third day. This promise vanished with all the rest in the wreck caused by His death. The disciples themselves forget all the consolations held out by Jesus so often and in particular on the night before His death (John 14–17). The gloom of despair settled upon their hearts. The task of the Risen Christ is to convince His own disciples that He is again alive and that the Kingdom of God has a future. He had been unable to get them to see that His Kingdom was spiritual and they took His death as the end of their hope of the political kingdom which they still looked for. The difficulty was very great, as we can see. But the first problem is the restoration of faith and hope.

The disciples were now all sceptics and pessimists and the Gospels all show this to be true. The accounts vary in many details concerning the

appearances of Jesus, but they give only frag-
mentary records of these days. They all insist on
the great fact that Jesus has risen from the now
empty grave and is alive and has appeared to His
disciples. Their independence strengthens their
witness. Modern doubt scouts the possibility of
resurrection of the body on scientific grounds and
all sorts of theories exist to explain away the actual
resurrection of the body of Jesus, like the swooning
of His body, the nervous fantasy of the women, the
psychic appearance of the soul (or the aura) of
Jesus, the invention of the story because the disciples wanted it. But no one of them explains the
revival of faith in the minds of these discouraged
men and women. Christianity is a fact, the greatest fact of history. Paul and the Gospel writers
explain the origin of Christianity as a religion on
the ground of the resurrection of Jesus in confirmation of His great claims to be the Son of God, the
Saviour of men. This interpretation has stood the
test of time and holds to-day, as the only adequate
explanation of the power of Christianity in the lives
of men.[1] John " recounts from his own experience

[1] Some of the most important discussions of the resurrection of Jesus are here given : Boardman, " Our Risen
King's Forty Days " (1902) ; Kennedy, " The Resurrection of Jesus Christ " (1895) ; Latham, " The Risen Master " (1901) ; Milligan, " The Resurrection of Our Lord "
(1886) ; Orr, " The Resurrection of Jesus " (1908) ;
Simpson, " Our Lord's Resurrection " (1906) ; Swete,
" The Appearances of Our Lord After the Passion " (1907) ;
Thorburn, " Resurrection Narratives and Modern Criti-

just those incidents which called out in the disciples
the fullness of belief triumphant over personal
sorrow, and common fear, and individual doubt"
(Westcott).

1. The First Visit of Mary Magdalene to the Tomb (20 : 1, 2).

John does not speak of the visit of the women to
see the sepulchre "late on the Sabbath" just before
sundown, the "dawn" of the first day (Matt. 28 : 1),
nor of the purchase of the spices after sundown (Mark
16 : 1). He makes no allusion to the other women
(Mark 16 : 1) who come with Mary Magdalene to
the tomb, "early, while it is yet dark" when they
start, though the sun is risen when they reach the
sepulchre (Mark 16 : 2). He is simply interested in
her part in the great event and passes by the rest.
It is probable at any rate that she ran on ahead of
the other women (because younger ?) when they see
"the stone taken away from [1] the tomb." This
of itself is cause enough for wonder. Without
waiting to look inside she runs "therefore" and
comes to Simon Peter (back again with the Beloved
Disciple) and John with her hasty interpretation of
the grave robbery, unspeakable shame, and calling
for the courage and skill of men to find the body of

cism " (1910) ; Westcott, " The Revelation of the Risen
Lord " (5th ed., 1891). A violent opponent of the resur-
rection is Lake, " Historical Evidence of the Resurrection of
Jesus Christ " (1907).

[1] ἐκ. Clean out to one side.

Jesus before it is further dishonoured. All this runs through the mind of Mary in a flash and she acts upon the impulse of the moment. The enemies of Christ have even tried to show despite to His corpse. In saying " we know not " Mary implies the presence of the other women with her.

2.   Peter and John at the Tomb (20 : 3–10).

There is a delicacy in this story that is very fine. These two disciples act in perfect keeping with their known characteristics. Peter " rushed out " [1] at once and then they ran side by side [2] to the tomb in their eagerness to set things straight. But John was fleeter of foot [3] and also finer in insight. He did come first [4] to the tomb, but he did not go on in, though he stoops down and looks at the clothes lying there. Peter now comes up and beholds [5] the clothes lying in orderly fashion just as John did. Peter went on in, impulsive as usual, to see the actual situation. John now overcame his shrinking by the example of Peter and went in also. But John, though first to come and last to go in, was the first to see into the meaning of the phenomena of the empty tomb and the orderly arrangement

---

[1] ἐξῆλθεν. Effective aorist.

[2] ἤρχοντο and ἔτρεχον (imperfects) picture them running ὁμοῦ (side by side).

[3] προέδραμεν τάχειον. Both προ- and the comparative and the aorist now.

[4] πρῶτος though only two. Common thus in the κοινή.

[5] θεωρεῖ. Intent looking. But βλέπει about John, merely glancing.

of the grave clothes. " He saw and believed." [1]
This is the great distinction [2] of the writer of the
Fourth Gospel, his marvellous spiritual vision, clear
and sure and piercing the empyrean of the eternal.
Hence he has given us " the spiritual gospel " as the
ancients said. Not yet did any of the disciples
understand the necessity [3] of the resurrection
though Jesus had told them repeatedly the fact, but
even that they could not take in (Luke 18 : 34).
Least of all had they associated any Scripture with
the subject. See Psalm 16 : 10 for the possible
reference. Jesus Himself will have to throw light
on the necessity of His death (Luke 24 : 26, 46).
But John, even in the midst of all the confusion of
the hour, saw that Mary Magdalene was wrong and
he, with a sensitive instinct, drew the logical conclusion that Jesus Himself had laid the clothes in
this orderly manner and hence had risen from the
dead. But it was not " proof," not even for Peter.
So they went away " by themselves," [4] for it was
useless as yet to talk to others.

3. Second Visit of Mary Magdalene (20 : 11–18).

Luke (24 : 8–11) tells of the message of the
women (including Mary Magdalene) to the Apostles, but does not separate her experience from the
rest. Their story was " as idle talk ; [5] and they dis-

---

[1] εἶδεν καὶ ἐπίστευσεν. Both aorists and instantaneous
action. Here still another verb for " seeing."

[2] Some manuscripts for Luke 24 : 12 give the visit of Peter
to the tomb.

[3] δεῖ.   [4] πρὸς αὐτούς.   [5] ὡσεί λῆρος.

believed them." Mark (16:9) in the disputed close of his Gospel tells of the appearance of Jesus to Mary first of all. But John alone gives in detail this wondrous scene between Jesus and Mary. There are many points on which one wishes for more light. Mary clearly did not see the angels when she was first at the tomb. Peter and John did not see the two angels (men) which the other women saw (Luke 24:4-8). But now, when she returns, Mary beholds two angels, one at the head and one at the foot of the place where the body of Jesus had lain (John 20:11 f.). The fact of angelic appearances here is no more difficult than elsewhere and is part of the problem of the relation of the spiritual world to the world of sense. The shepherds heard the angels sing at the birth of Jesus as these women saw the angels who testify of His resurrection from the grave. Mary is still troubled over her idea of the grave robbery (20:13). Clearly John's Gospel lends no support to the theory that the women, Mary Magdalene in particular, had hallucinations and led the apostles to believe that Jesus was alive. The women are presented as not expecting to see Jesus alive and the apostles disbelieved their story when they told it. The angels threw no light on the situation for Mary. First of all mortals (save the guard) she saw the Risen Christ and did not recognize Him. There are various reasons for her ignorance. She had been weeping. She was in utter anguish over the thought of the grave robbery. She was in the garden and the natural man to appear was the gardener. Besides, Jesus was not quite as He was before His death. He appeared " in another form" (Mark 16 : 12) to the two disciples going to Emmaus " whose eyes were holden" (Luke 24 : 16). Jesus was able to throw a veil over the eyes of those whom He did not wish to recognize Him. But Mary's address to the supposed gardener shows that she now hopes that he has removed the body of Jesus which she craves the duty of caring for. But one word from Jesus is all that is needed to dispel the mist from the eyes of Mary. It is her name on His lips as of old. In the rush of emotion she can only say : " Rabboni " (" My Master ") in recognition. She evidently tries to take hold of Him, to cling[1] to Him and Jesus forbids her, for, He explains, He is only here for a short time before He ascends to " my Father and your Father, and my God and your God." He did allow the other women later to take hold of His feet in worship (Matt. 28 : 9), but merely human fellowship was not to be resumed. But Jesus shows in His very language the highest sense of spiritual fellowship with Mary and the rest. Jesus bade her go to His brethren and tell them. She had a marvellous message, one that they needed and really longed to hear. Mary was able to say first of all men : " I have seen the Lord,"[2] the Risen Lord. But they evidently disbelieved her. She was only Mary who once had seven demons. Was she to be

---

[1] μή μου ἅπτου. Present tense. He bids her to cease clinging to Him.   [2] Ἑώρακα τὸν κύριον.

believed in a matter like this? Where was John's
instinct?

4. The Meeting the First Sunday Night (20 : 19–25).

John's narrative corroborates in a most important
manner that of the Synoptics and in particular the
wonderful story in Luke 24 : 13–35, the walk of the
unrecognized Christ with two disciples to their
home in Emmaus. Renan calls this the most
beautiful story in all the world. It is quite too
beautiful to be invented by a truth-loving historian
like Luke, though it is told with matchless skill.
But our interest here is in the sequel, for Luke
represents these two disciples, once their eyes are
opened, as hurrying back to Jerusalem to tell the
disciples the glorious news, only to find them as-
sembled, probably in that same Upper Room of precious associations, and already convinced of the fact
of the resurrection of Jesus because " he hath appeared [1] to Simon " (Luke 24 : 34). They tell their
story to the joy of all. It is at this juncture (Luke
24 : 36) that John takes up the story. He adds a
few details to the account in Mark and Luke. He
uses Roman time, " evening, on that day, the first
day of the week." He explains that the door was
shut for fear of the Jews. The disciples still feel
like hunted birds. John speaks of the circumstance to show that the appearance is a miracle and
also to explain something of the nature of the resur-

[1] ὤφθη. The usual word and means actual sight.

rection body of Jesus which passes through closed doors, although His hands and His side (20 : 20) bear the marks of the nails and the spear. Luke (24 : 42) tells of His eating a piece of broiled fish to remove the disbelief of the disciples at the sudden apparition. John shows how they did come to rejoice at the sight of the Lord. Twice (20 : 19, 21) Jesus bestows " peace " on the disciples, the first time to restore confidence, the second time to prepare for work (Westcott). The commission here given is on a par with that in Matthew 28 : 16–20 and like that is addressed to all the disciples present (Luke 24 : 33), not to the Apostles alone. The breathing of the Holy Spirit was symbolic of the very word " spirit " (breath, wind) and probably suggests quickening into new apprehension (cf. Gen. 2 : 7) preparatory to the endowment at Pentecost (Westcott). The assumption of divine prerogatives and authority here is precisely as in Matthew 28 : 16–20. Jesus is like a general planning a campaign, only this one is for the conquest of the world. He commands them to receive[1] the Holy Spirit.

The forgiveness (remission) of sin here put in the hands of Christ's people is not the power of absolution, but the declaration of the fact and the terms by which it is obtained (20 : 23). Luke in the last commission (24 : 47) reports Jesus as saying " that repentance and remission of sins should be preached

---

[1] $\lambda\acute{\alpha}\beta\varepsilon\tau\grave{\varepsilon}$. Take. Each man has to exercise his own choice in this great matter.

in his name into all nations." This is clearly what
Jesus means in John. He uses a rabbinical mode
of speech, but He no more means to impart to men
the power of bestowing forgiveness than He meant
to confer on Peter the power to regulate the Kingdom of God (Matt. 16 : 18 f.). The disciples are to
bring forgiveness to men by the message of life
through Christ. The dread power of sin is seen
precisely in the fearful cost of forgiveness. The
price of redemption is the blood of Jesus and forgiveness is only possible by the grace of God, for
nature knows no forgiveness of the violation of her
laws without penalty. John closes this incident
with the statement that Thomas was absent from
this first gathering of the disciples after the resurrection of Jesus. We do not know why he was not
there, but he was obdurate and even cynical in his
doubt of the story of the disciples, as they had been
towards the report of the women. When they gave
details, he retorted that he required the same items
to convince him. Thus the first effort of the disciples to convince one of their own number failed.
They evidently needed more skill and power from
the Holy Spirit if they were to carry out the commission just given them by Jesus.

5. **The Meeting the Second Sunday Night**
(20 : 26–29).

Things could never again be as they had been.
Jesus had appeared to various individuals and once
to the group on that first Sunday night. The

clouds were forever lifted from their hearts. Some still doubted, like Thomas, and others later when they first saw Jesus as was natural (Matt. 28 : 17). But this little band of men and women were knit together in a hallowed experience that changed the horizon of the world for them. Jesus is alive. The Kingdom is not over. All is not lost. All is true that they had hoped and more, though new and strange. They are not yet ready to go forward, for He Himself has an appointed meeting with them on the mountain in Galilee. So they wait with fluttering hearts. On this second night they gather as a matter of course and they persuade Thomas to come this time. They had no assurance that Jesus was to appear to them on this night, but it will do them good to meet together and talk over the tremendous import of the new turn in their life as followers of Jesus. They are still afraid of the Jews and the doors are shut as before. Jesus suddenly stepped[1] into the midst and gave the greeting of peace (*shalōm*). But the presence of Thomas leads Jesus to accept his challenge. Thomas was an honest man, if cautious, and a noble one. His confession reaches the highest plane of the Gospels. He said simply : " My Lord and my God." [2] With these words vanished all doubt and came full surrender and faith. Jesus accepted his homage, but

---

[1] ἔστη.

[2] ὁ κύριός μου καὶ ὁ θεός μου. The nominative form is common in the vocative. The way Jesus received his words proves that it is address, not exclamation.

took pains to point out that he had missed the opportunity for the highest faith in not believing without sight. These words lingered in the memory of Peter also (1 Peter 1 : 8) and this highest type of faith is open to us all to-day.

6. The Author's Ideal (20: 30, 31).

The book seems finished for it is hardly possible to rise above the confession of Thomas. I am inclined to think that John did stop at this point and at a later time added chapter 21 as an Epilogue. He looks back upon his task with an author's feeling of incompleteness, almost of dissatisfaction. He has produced the noblest book ever written by man, but does not seem to know it. He is conscious of the many other signs that Jesus did which he knows and cannot record for lack of space. He has not tried to tell all that he knows. He has frankly written with purpose and has made a selection out of the vast material at his disposal. His purpose is the noblest that is possible for any author. He wants his readers to believe that Jesus is in reality the Christ, the Son of God, not as a mere theological dictum or shibboleth of orthodoxy, but that by believing they may have life. This can only come to them in the name and power of this same Son of God whose coming to earth he has proven in this book. The wish is a prayer and a hope.

7. By the Beloved Lake (21 : 1–23).

If this is an epilogue or appendix, as I think it is,

it in no way interferes with the aim and spirit of
the book to which it is added. In a beautiful way
it illustrates the life of the disciples during the great
forty days when Jesus appeared to them at intervals.[1]
It is probable that this appendix was added by John
because of a current misapprehension of a saying
of Jesus about the longevity of the beloved disciple
(21 : 20–23) which he corrects. The style is precisely that of the rest of the Gospel. The chapter
reveals still further the glory of the Risen Christ.
This further manifestation, besides those at Jerusalem, took place at the Sea of Tiberias whither seven
of the Apostles had gone—while waiting for the
appointment on the mountain in Galilee. This
appearance was a surprise, as all of them were, save
the one arranged by Jesus just mentioned. The
names of five are given, but two are not. Hence it
is possible that the beloved disciple (21 : 7) is one
of these two instead of John, one of the sons of
Zebedee. But the other arguments (see Chapter I)
make it highly probable that the author of the book
is John, who is also the beloved disciple. Fishing
was once the vocation of some of these men and
now it is their avocation. Peter's impulse rallies
the rest to the enterprise which they probably
enjoy in spite of catching nothing. Fellowship is a
large part of the pleasure of fishing. But the picture of Jesus standing on the shore in the haze of
the early dawn is one that John never forgot
through the long years. He had taught them how

[1] Acts 1 : 3. δι᾽ ἡμερῶν τεσσεράκοντα ὀπτανόμενος.

to catch fish before, as John is the first to recall
with the quick conclusion : " It is the Lord " (21 : 7).
But Peter acts first again and soon they are all on
shore counting the one hundred and fifty-three big
fishes as they leaped about in the net. There is no
need now to ask : " Who art thou ? " They all
know by common instinct that it is the Lord
(21 : 12). So they have a breakfast with Jesus with
beating hearts, this third time that Jesus has manifested Himself to a group of the disciples.

But John is not done with the incident. Jesus turns
to Peter and asks him three times if he loves Him, one
time for each denial. This time also it is early dawn
and by a fire of coals. Peter had boasted of his great
love above all others, but now he drops that. So Jesus
repeats the question without the " more than these."
The third time Jesus changes His verb [1] to that of
Peter as if to challenge even this humble claim.

The heart of Peter is very humble now and all
boasting is gone. He trusts Jesus with His un-
bounded knowledge (21 : 17) to understand the sincerity of his love, however poorly he has shown it.
Jesus had said that when Peter had turned he must
stablish his brethren (Luke 22 : 32). Now Jesus
three times charges him to feed [2] and to shepherd [3]

---

[1] From ἀγαπάω to φιλέω. No iron-clad distinction can
be drawn between these two verbs. Φιλέω is to love as a
friend (affection of the heart like *amo*) while ἀγαπάω (like
diligo) is the higher love of choice. But the words are often
used interchangeably, only here the distinction is drawn.

[1] βόσκε.   [2] ποίμαινε.

His lambs. It is a great task and Peter cherishes it
(cf. 1 Peter 5 : 2 f.). Peter had once boasted of his
readiness to die for Jesus and had then denied Him.
But now he is to have a martyr's crown after all
(21 : 18 f.) if he will only follow Jesus.

The query of Peter about the fate of John who
came up at this moment is quite of a piece with
Peter's quick and impetuous nature. But the sharp
rebuke of Jesus by no means indicates that John
was to live till Jesus returned to earth at the end
(21 : 20–23). John himself is now old and his eyes
are longing for the Coming of Jesus, but he denies
this false interpretation of the saying.

8. Addendum (21 : 24 f.).

Dods argues that John himself could very well
have written verse 24 since he identifies himself as
the witness of the piercing of the side of Jesus
(19 : 35). That is true as a possibility, but the
probability is quite the other way. The use of the
plural " we know " is not decisive in itself, but in
contrast with " I think " in verse 25 the probability
is greatly increased. The hyperbole in verse 25 is
simply an expansion of 20 : 30. As John closes the
epilogue he is overwhelmed afresh with the magni-
tude of the work of Jesus Christ. There is wonder
in each deed and glory in every logion that he spoke.
No one has ever written a full life of Christ. No
one can ever do it. But let us thank God for what
has been written and for the expanding power of
Christ through the ages (Acts 1 : 1) and His abid-

ing presence in our own hearts (John 14 : 23).
Some day we shall see Him as He is and be, wonder of wonders, somewhat like Him (1 John 3 : 2).
Jesus not only reveals God to men, but in the end
makes us like God.

Some Books on John's Gospel

*(Besides Introductions to the New Testament
and General Commentaries)*

Abbott, Ezra, On the Authorship of the Fourth Gospel.
1880.

Abbott, E. A., Johannine Grammar. 1906.

Abbott, E. A., Johannine Vocabulary. 1905.

Ackwith, The Historical Value of the Fourth Gospel.
1910.

Appel, Die Echtheit des Johannesevangeliums. 1915.

Bacon, The Fourth Gospel in Research and Debate.
1910.

Baldensperger, Der Prolog des vierten Evangeliums.
1898.

Barth, The Gospel of John and the Synoptic Gospels.
1907.

Bauer, Hand-Commentar von Holtzmann. 3d ed.
1908.

Benham, St. John and His Work.

Blass, Evangelium Secundum Johannes. 1902.

Candler, Practical Studies in the Gospel of John. 3 vols.
1912–1915.

Carr, Gospel of St. John. 1904.

Chapman, John the Presbyter and the Fourth Gospel.
1911.

Clemen, Die Entstehung des Johannesevangeliums. 1912.

Culross, John Whom Jesus Loved. 1878.

Delff, Das vierte Evangelium wiedergestellt. 1890.

Delff, Neue Beiträge zur Kritik und Erklärung des vierten
Evangeliums. 1890.

Dods, Gospel of John. 2 vols. in Expositor's Bible. 1891.

Dods, Gospel of John in Expositor's Greek Testament. 1902.

Drummond, An Inquiry into the Character and Authorship of the Fourth Gospel. 1904.

Evans, St. John the Author of the Fourth Gospel. 1888.

Fouard, S. Jean et la fin de l'âge apostolique. 1904.

Gardner, The Ephesian Gospel. 1915.

Gloag, Life of St. John. 1891.

Göbel, Die Reden des Herrn nach Johannes. 2 vols. 1906–1910.

Godet, Commentary on the Gospel of St. John. 2 vols. 1886–1890.

Gordon, Quiet Talks on the Gospel of John.

Gregory, Wellhausen und Johannes. 1910.

Grill, Untersuchungen über die Entstehung des vierten Evangeliums. 1902.

Harnack, Ueber das Verhältniss des Prologs des vierten Evangeliums zum ganzen Werke. 1892.

Hovey, Gospel of John in American Commentary. 1885.

Inge, The Historical Value of the Fourth Gospel (Cambridge Biblical Essays). 1909.

Jackson, The Fourth Gospel and Some Recent German Criticisms. 1906.

Johnstone, The Philosophy of the Fourth Gospel. 1909.

Krenkel, Apostel Johannes. 1897.

Kreyenbühl, Neue Lösung des Johanneischen Frage. 1905.

Lepin, L'Origine du Quatrième 'Evangile. 1907.

Lewis, Disarrangements in the Fourth Gospel. 1910.

Lias, Doctrinal System of St. John. 1875.

Lightfoot, Essay on in Biblical Essays. 1893.

Lock, The Literary Method of the Fourth Gospel (*Hibbert Journal*, October, 1916).

Loisy, Le Quatrième 'Evangile. 1903.

Lowrie, The Doctrine of John. 1895.

Lutgert, Johannes Christologie.

Luthardt, St. John the Author of the Fourth Gospel. 1875.

Matheson, St. John's Portrait of Christ. 1910.

McClymont, Gospel of John in the New Century Bible. 1901.

McDonald, Life and Writings of St. John. 1877.

Milligan and Moulton, Gospel of John in Schaff's Commentary, 1895.

Niese, Das Leben des heiligen Johannes. 1878.

Overbeck, Das Johannesevangelium. 1911.

Peyton, The Memorabilia of Jesus.

Plummer, Cambridge Greek Testament. Gospel of John. 1893.

Reynolds, Pulpit Commentary-Gospel of John. 3 vols. 1887–1888.

Richmond, The Gospel of the Rejection. 1906.

Robinson, Historical Character of St. John's Gospel.

Sanday, The Criticism of the Fourth Gospel. 1905.

Schmiedel, The Johannine Writings. 1908.

Schwartz, Ueber den Tod der Söhne Zebedai. 1904.

Scott, The Fourth Gospel: Its Purpose and Theology. 1906.

Scott, The Historical and Religious Value of the Fourth Gospel. 1909.

Scott, The Hellenistic Mysticism of the Fourth Gospel (*American Journal of Theology*, July, 1916).

Scott-Moncrieff, St. John, Apostle, Evangelist, and Prophet. 1909.

Sears, The Fourth Gospel the Heart of Christ. 1872.

Sense, A Free Inquiry into the Authorship of the Fourth Gospel.

Smith, J. R., The Teaching of the Fourth Gospel. 1903.

Speer, The Greatest Book in the World. 1915.

Spitta, Das Johannesevangelium als Quelle der Geschichte Jesu. 1909.

Stalker, The Two St. Johns. 1895.

Stanton, Part I of The Gospels as Historical Documents. 1903.

Stevens, Johannine Theology. 1894.

Watkins, Modern Criticism Considered in Its Relation to the Fourth Gospel. 1890.

Watson, The Mysticism of St. John's Gospel. 1916.

Weiss, B., Der Johanneische Lehrbegriff. 1882.

Weiss, B., Meyer-Komm. 9th ed. 1902.

Wellhausen, Das Evangelium Johannis. 1908.

Wendt, The Gospel According to St. John : An Inquiry into its Genesis and Historical Value. 1902.

Wendt, Die Schichten im vierten Evangelium. 1911.

Westcott, Commentary on the Gospel of St. John. 2 vols. 1908.

Whitelaw, The Gospel of John. 1888.

Worsley, The Fourth Gospel and the Synoptists. 1909.

Wrede, Charakter und Tendenz des Johannesevangeliums. 1903.

Zahn, Zahn Komm. 1909.

Printed in the United States of America

WAYNE WHIPPLE

The Story-Life of the Son of Man

8vo, illustrated, net $2.50.

"A literary mosaic, consisting of quotations from a great number of writers concerning all the events of the Gospels. The sub-title accurately describes its contents. That sub-title is 'Nearly a thousand stories from sacred and secular sources in a continuous and complete chronicle of the earth life of the Saviour.' The book was prepared for the general reader, but will be valuable to minister, teacher and student. There are many full-page engravings from historic paintings and sacred originals, some reproduced for the first time."—*Christian Observer.*

GAIUS GLENN ATKINS, D.D.

Pilgrims of the Lonely Road

12mo, cloth, net $1.50.

"A rare book for its style, its theme and the richness of its insight. Seldom is seen a book of more exquisite grace of diction—happy surprises of phrase, and lovely lengths of haunting prose to delight the eye. Each of the great pilgrim's studies is followed step by step along the lonely way of the soul in its quest of light, toward the common goal of all—union with the eternal."—*Chicago Record-Herald.*

S. D. GORDON

Quiet Talks on Following The Christ

12mo, cloth, net 75c.

"This volume is well calculated to aid in Christian life, to give strength, courage and light on difficult problems. It grips one's very life, brings one face to face with God's word, ways of understanding it and, even its every day application. It is plain, clear, direct, no confusion of dark sentences."—*Bapt. Observer.*

G. CAMPBELL MORGAN, D.D.

The Teaching of Christ

A Companion Volume to "The Crises of The Christ." 8vo, cloth, net $1.50.

"One does not read far before he is amazed at the clear and logical grasp Dr. Morgan has upon divine truths. Could a copy of this book, with its marvelous insight, its straightforwardness, its masterly appeal, be placed in the hands of our church leaders, it would go far toward negativing the spiritual barrenness of destructive criticism. Here is a work that may profitably occupy a prominent place in the minister's library."—*Augsburg Teacher.*

ZEPHINE HUMPHREY

The Edge of the Woods And Other Papers

12mo, cloth, net $1.25.

"Sane optimism, an appreciation of the beautiful and a delicate humor pervades the book which is one for lovers of real literature to enjoy."—*Pittsburgh Post.*

EDWARD AUGUSTUS GEORGE

The Twelve : Apostolic Types of Christian Men

12mo, cloth, net $1.00

"Under his living touch the apostles seem very much like the men we know and their problems not dissimilar to our own."—*Congregationalist.*

PROF. W. G. MOOREHEAD

OUTLINE STUDIES in the NEW TESTAMENT SERIES

The Catholic Epistles and Revelation

In One Volume. *New Edition.* 12mo, net $1.20

Containing James, I and II Peter, I, II and III John, and Jude, and the Book of Revelation.

ALEXANDER CRUDEN

Complete Concordance

Large 8vo, cloth, net $1.00.

New Unabridged Edition, with the Table of Proper Names entirely revised and mistranslations in the meanings corrected, many suggestive notes.

WILLIAM SMITH, LL.D.

A Dictionary of the Bible

Its Antiquities, Biography, Geography and Natural History, with Numerous Illustrations and Maps. *A New Worker's Edition.* 776 pages. Net $1.00.

NEW THIN PAPER EDITION

The Boy Scouts' Twentieth Century New Testament

Officially authorized by the Boy Scouts' of America. New Thin Paper Edition.

181. 16mo, khaki cloth, net 85c.

182. 16mo, ooze leather, khaki color, net $1.50.

Contains an introduction by the Executive Board, the Scouts' Oath, and the Scouts' Law.

HENRY T. SELL, D.D. (Editor)   *Author of Sell's Bible Studies*

XX Century Story of the Christ

12mo, cloth, *in press.*

From the text of The Twentieth Century New Testament, Dr. Sell has completed a Harmony of The Gospels which, while studiously avoiding repetition omits no important word in the fourfold record of the earthly life and teaching of our Lord. He has done his work well, and the result is a compilation specially designed and adapted for the use of the average reader

JOHN HENRY JOWETT

My Daily Meditation for the Circling Year

12mo, cloth, net $1.25.

A series of choice, tabloid talks—a spiritual meditation for every day in the year. Dr. Jowett points every word of these brief expositions so that it tells, while the lessons he seeks to convey are so propounded as to enter the understanding of his readers along a pathway of light. The whole volume is of true mintage, bearing the impress of Dr. Jowett's ripest thought and fruitful mind.

S. D. GORDON

Quiet Talks About the Crowned Christ

12mo, cloth, net 75c.

After many years' study of the one book of the Bible devoted to the subject of the crowned Christ—the Revelation of John—Mr. Gordon has put these latest talks together. No book of the sixty-six has seemed so much like a riddle, and set so many guessing. Mr. Gordon, however, holds the deep conviction that it is wholly a *practical book,* and concerned wholly with our practical daily lives.

F. B. MEYER, B.A.

My Daily Prayer

A Short Supplication for Every Day in the Year. 32mo, leather, net 35c; cloth, net 25c.

"This is a tiny volume, in the 'Yet Another Day' series, and contains a brief prayer for each day in the year. Some of the petitions contain only one sentence, but each one is simple, pertinent, and helpful."—*Zion's Herald.*

GEORGE MATHESON

Day Unto Day

A Brief Prayer for Every Day. *New Edition.* 16mo, cloth, net 50c.

These choice prayers will be valued by the Christian world for the stimulus, inspiration, and wide spiritual outlook which have made the memory of their author a cherished possession.

HENRY WARD BEECHER

A Book of Public Prayer

12mo, cloth, net 75c.

"A distinct addition to our devotional literature. It is good for private reading; but would be especially valuable for ministers as an aid to the difficult, but immensely important, service of voicing the petitions of a congregation in public prayer."—*Standard.*

ALBERT L. VAIL

Portraiture of Jesus in the Gospels

12mo, cloth, net 75c.

A fourfold portrait of Jesus as He stands out on the can-vas of each of the Four Gospels. The varying and dis-tinctive shadings of the four pictures, are not, Mr. Vail con-tends, a matter of accident but of Divine arrangement and design. Our Lord is thus presented in a fourfold aspect in order that His appeal to various classes of mankind might be the more manifold.

FRANK E. WILSON, B.D.

Contrasts in the Character of Christ

12mo, cloth, net $1.00.

Jesus Christ is still the key to the modern situation. No matter what "up-to-date" methods of reform and reclamation spring to life, the message of Christ is the one great solution of the problems confronting humanity. From this position Dr. Wilson leads his readers to a contemplation of an abid-ing Jesus, and to a consideration of many modern points of contact contained in His all-sufficient Gospel.

WILLIAM BRUCE DOYLE

The Holy Family

As Viewed and Viewing in His Unfolding Minis-try. 12mo, cloth, net 75c.

This book covers new ground; for although separate sketches of individual members of Joseph's family abound, a study of the family group as a whole,—one marked with satis-factory detail remained to be furnished. This has been ably supplied. The author's work is everywhere suffused with reverence, as becometh one writing of some of the most en-deared traditions cherished by the human race.

BOOKLETS

DAVID DE FOREST BURRELL   _Author of "The Gift"_

The Lost Star

An Idyll of the Desert. 16mo, net 25c.

An appealing story of a Shepherd's search for the Star. It is so tender, so sweet, so Christ-like, it is sure to captivate everyone.